Mr & Mrs Smith
Hotel Collection

UK/Ireland
Volume 2

FOR TW

Who says the sequel is never as thrilling? Eight years after we first started researching our inaugural UK/Ireland guidebook, we're thrilled to present an updated edition of our rather dazzling follow-up. Why the long wait? Simple: we wanted to impress you with a completely fresh, knock-out collection of hotels with that all-important 'wow' factor. Among a starry array of super-luxe country retreats, boutique bed and breakfasts and hot new city stays, you'll recognise a few familiar façades: these Smith favourites have once again earned a special mention thanks to a new spa-enhanced or bedroom-boosted lease of life. And, once again, we've done our homework to bring you those in-the-know details you can't find anywhere else, highlighting the most seductive rooms, the finest local dining, and the only activities worth getting out of bed for...

When Mr & Mrs Smith first got together, the label 'boutique' was still a young one. Now that the bandwagon is buckling under the weight of these would-be designer boltholes, we at Smith HQ are inundated with proposals – making our rigorous selection process more crucial than ever. As always, we've loved having an illustrious panel of taste-makers and design connoisseurs to help us roadtest this new collection (including fashion scribe Jess Cartner-Morley, radio raconteur Shaun Keaveny and Serena Rees, creator of Agent Provocateur). And, thanks to regular feedback from Smith members, we're able to keep an eye on our hotels, so we know they're all still meeting our sky-high expectations.

We've circumnavigated the globe in our hunt for hip hideaways: there are now more than 850 recommendations in our international collection at www.mrandmrssmith.com, and we have offices in New York and Melbourne. Not only can you book online with us for free, but we also guarantee that you'll get the best room rates available; if you prefer doing things over the phone, you can always speak to a friendly member of our helpful Travel Team. As a Smith cardholder, you get exclusive offers on hotels, travel, shopping and you earn money back on each booking; simply turn the page for details of your year's free membership.

So, next time you're planning an escape, get yourself in the mood by lying back with your copy of *Mr & Mrs Smith*, and thinking of England, Ireland, Scotland and Wales... And rest assured – you'll soon be having the time of your life.

Best wishes and bon voyage,

Mr & Mrs Smith

(take)

advantage of us

This is your own personal Smithcard, which entitles you to six months' free membership. The moment you register it, you can access the members' area of our website, and find out about exclusive last-minute offers from our hotels. The card also provides members-only privileges – such as a free bottle of champagne on arrival, spa treats, late check-out and more – when you book hotels through us. Look out for the *Smith* at the end of each hotel review.

A Mr & Mrs Smith membership card should be affixed here.
If it has been removed, you can still buy the book and we will send you a replacement card. Please send proof of purchase, with a return address, to either:

LONDON
2nd Floor
334 Chiswick High Road
London W4 5TA
United Kingdom

NEW YORK
580 Broadway
Suite 1202
New York NY 10012
United States

MELBOURNE
Level 1
137 Flinders Lane
Melbourne VIC 3000
Australia

REGISTER NOW

To start getting money back every time you book, hotel offers and exclusive travel benefits, activate your BlackSmith card by registering online at www.mrandmrssmith.com/register-card or by ringing one of the numbers below (it only takes a minute).

ROOM SERVICE

Activate your membership today, and you will also receive our fantastic monthly newsletter *Room Service*. It's packed with news, travel tips, even more offers, and great competitions. We promise not to bombard you with communications, or pass on your details to third parties – this is strictly between you and us.

MONEY BACK WITH EVERY BOOKING

Depending on your membership level, Mr & Mrs Smith credits up to five per cent of your bookings to a special member's account.

AND THERE'S MORE?

If all this isn't enough, you can even get access to VIP airport lounges, automatic room upgrades, flight and car-hire offers, and your own dedicated travel consultant, simply by upgrading your membership to SilverSmith or GoldSmith. Visit www.mrandmrssmith.com for more details.

ON CALL

Thanks to our global Travel Team, Mr & Mrs Smith operates a 24-hour travel service five days a week. Ring any of the numbers below to activate your membership today, and start planning your first Smith adventure.

In the UK, ring 0845 034 0700
US and Canada, call toll-free on 1 800 464 2040
In Australia, call 1300 896627

In New Zealand, call 0800 986671
From anywhere in Asia, ring +61 3 8648 8871*
From elsewhere in the world, ring +44 20 8987 6970

*Also check www.mrandmrssmith.com/contact for new free or local call numbers from territories in Asia.
Small print: all offers are dependent on availability and subject to change.

(contents)

(at a glance)

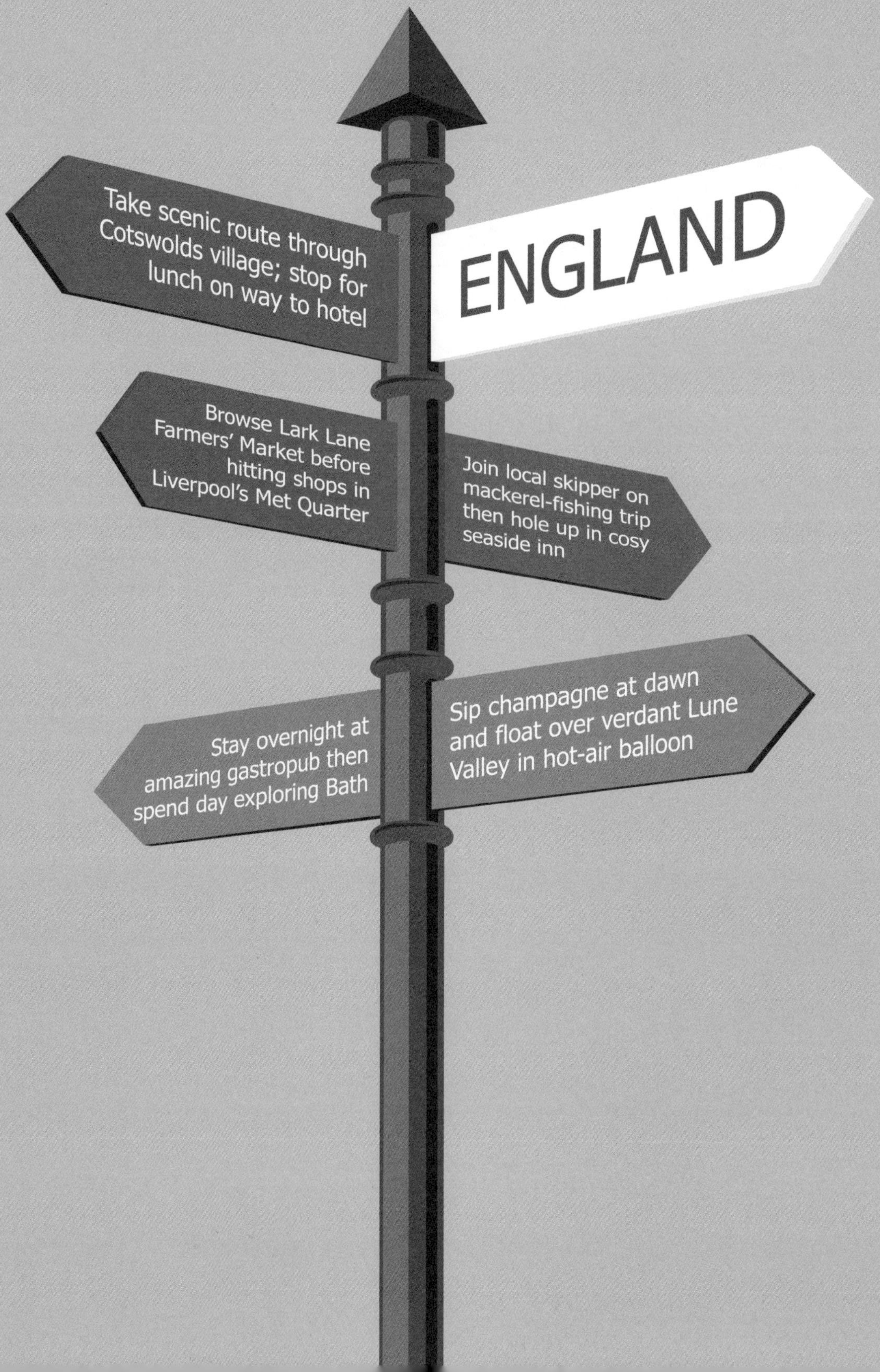
ENGLAND
Take scenic route through Cotswolds village; stop for lunch on way to hotel
Browse Lark Lane Farmers' Market before hitting shops in Liverpool's Met Quarter
Join local skipper on mackerel-fishing trip then hole up in cosy seaside inn
Stay overnight at amazing gastropub then spend day exploring Bath
Sip champagne at dawn and float over verdant Lune Valley in hot-air balloon

ENGLAND

Cornwall
Driftwood

The Cotswolds
Barnsley House
Cotswold House
Lower Slaughter Manor
Rectory Hotel
Thirty Two

Cumbria
Hipping Hall

Devon
Hotel Endsleigh
Whitehouse

Dorset
The Bull Hotel

East Sussex
The George in Rye
Square

Hampshire
Lime Wood

Liverpool
Hope Street Hotel

London
Bingham
Haymarket Hotel
High Road House

Norfolk
Strattons

Northeast Somerset
Babington House
The Wheatsheaf

Peak District
The Peacock at Rowsley

Suffolk
Tuddenham Mill

ENGLAND

CORNWALL

COASTLINE Rocky shores and rolling surf
COAST LIFE Crest of a wave; catch of the day

With its soft sand beaches, hot summer sun and spectacularly noisy waves, Cornwall is the stuff of perfect childhood holidays. This remote and beautiful part of the British Isles has won back a new generation of devotees who have discovered its unique magic (and almost sub-tropical micro-climate). A few halcyon days here will offer all the stupendous sea views, peaceful beaches and laid-back living you could want, and the fabulously fresh seafood means a gastronomic treat lies in every cove; celebrated chefs have moved to the region and vie for your attention among the beachfront shellfish shacks, the country inns and traditional tearooms. There's plenty to help you work up an appetite, including clifftop walks, art galleries and sailing; and the surfing is perhaps the best in the UK. Whether you join the crowds in high summer or find some perfect solitude out of season, you're sure to fall under Cornwall's powerful spell.

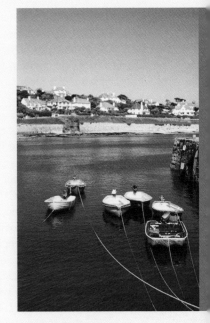

GETTING THERE

Planes Newquay International (www.newquay-airport.co.uk), Cornwall's main airport, has flights from Manchester (BMI Baby), and London Stansted (Ryanair). Cornwall has its own airline, Air Southwest, which flies from Bristol, Manchester, Leeds and Dublin, among others.

Trains The journey to the South West from London Paddington takes between four and five hours. First Great Western offers the very civilised Night Riviera Sleeper to Penzance, departing London shortly before midnight and arriving at around 8am; to book, ring 0845 700 0125.

Automobiles The five- or six-hour drive to Cornwall from London, along the M4 and M5 (or via the slower but more scenic A303) is something either to savour or curse. Once in Cornwall, you'll pretty much need a car; roads can be hellishly congested in the summer, so allow extra time.

LOCAL KNOWLEDGE

Taxis Cabs are thin on the ground, so ask your hotel for a number and book ahead if you can. Ring 01726 832676 for Fowey Taxi Service; Truro Taxi Cab Co is on 01872 321321.

Packing tips The beaches of Cornwall are often pounded by Atlantic breakers, making this county the centre of Britain's surf culture. If this is your thing, pack plenty of Billabong, Ripcurl and Oxbow.

Recommended reads 'Last night I dreamt I went to Manderley again...' For rich Cornish romance and drama, read Daphne du Maurier's dark, fabulously vivid novel *Rebecca*. Another Cornwall-set classic is Mary Wesley's *The Camomile Lawn*. Before attempting Cornish polymath DM Thomas's dream-like *The White Hotel*, dip into *Dear Shadows*, his recent poetry collection.

Local specialities High-calorie treats abound, none messier than a Cornish cream tea of scones, jam and clotted cream. As well as an authentic (Cornish) pasty from Philps Bakery in Hayle (01736 755661), and fish 'n' chips from Rick Stein's Padstow chippie, don't leave without trying raisin-studded saffron cake; stargazy pie – a fish dish served with the heads and tails poking up through a pastry crust; and yarg, a nettle-wrapped cheese based on a 13th-century recipe, now made only by Lynher Dairies (www.cornishyarg.co.uk).

Perfect picnic The headlands overlooking Lantic Bay east of the Fowey (pronounced 'Foy') estuary are ideal on a warm day; with freshly baked bread and West Country delicacies, Tiffins Delicatessen on Fowey's Fore Street

(01726 832322) can't be beaten for picnic fixings. On the north coast, head for the clifftop on the Rumps walk near Polzeath, stopping for supplies at Di's Dairy and Pantry in Rock on the way (01208 863531).

And... The rabble-rousing chant 'Oggy, Oggy, Oggy!' – often heard at rugby matches, Scout meetings, and even once at the Oscars when Catherine Zeta-Jones collected hers – comes from a Cornish folk song; oggy is a slang term for a pasty.

WORTH GETTING OUT OF BED FOR

Viewpoint Watch the sun set beyond Longships Lighthouse at Land's End. At the other end of the county, Kit Hill, between Tavistock and Liskeard, gives views all the way to both the north and south coasts.

Arts and culture In summer, the open-air Minack Theatre, high on the cliffs near Porthcurno, makes the most of its wild-seas backdrop (www.minack.com). Near St Austell, the Eden Project (www.edenproject.com) makes you feel like an excited kid again – even on a rainy day, inside the conservatory biomes it's totally tropical. Tate St Ives by Porthmeor beach has a collection of work by contemporary British artists (www.tate.org.uk/stives), but don't miss its sister museum on Barnoon Hill, dedicated to Barbara Hepworth (01736 796226). The magnificent sculpture garden is laid out according to her original plans.

Activities North Cornwall has excellent surf beaches; Newquay's Extreme Academy will get you surfing as well as dirt-boarding and kite buggying (01637 860840). There's water-skiing on the estuary with the Camel Ski School in Rock (01208 862727); and Adventure Cornwall offers coastal kayaking as well as climbing on Bodmin Moor (01726 870844). With Fowey River Sailing, you can take to the water in a traditional wooden dinghy (01208 873721).

Daytripper Hop over to the Isles of Scilly, an archipelago of 140 tiny, rocky islands – only five inhabited – some 28 miles off Cornwall's tip. Once there, take boat trips, snorkel with seals (www.scillydiving.com), laze on the beach or eat your way around the seafood cafés of St Mary's. Get there by plane from Newquay or Land's End with Skybus (www.skybus.co.uk), or by helicopter from Penzance (www.islesofscillyhelicopter.com).

Children Take tweenagers boarding at the Fistral Beach Surf School in Newquay (www.fistralbeachsurfschool.co. uk), and younger children to the Crealy Adventure Park near Wadebridge, which has fairground rides and a petting zoo (www.crealy.co.uk). Best known for its

colourful parrots, Paradise Park near St Ives also has otters and shrieking barn owls (www.paradisepark.org.uk).

Walks One of the prettiest options is the Hall Walk, a looping two-mile trail around the Fowey estuary that requires a couple of ferry hops to complete. The clifftops south of Bude, with their spectacular rock formations, make for a dramatic trek. The Lost Gardens of Heligan in St Austell (www.heligan.com), a Victorian estate with pools, grottos and vegetable gardens, provides a gentler stroll.

Shopping There are several farmers' markets in the region; have a wander at the Truro market at Lemon Quay on Wednesdays and Saturdays, or the Tuesday morning market in central Falmouth. The New Gallery in Portscatho (01872 580445) and Padstow Gallery (01841 532242) are excellent art-hunting grounds, as are the smaller dealerships in Veryan, Tregony and St Just in Roseland. Mrs Smiths will love Onda, the sleek boutique at St Mawes' Hotel Tresanton (01326 270456).

Something for nothing The evocative ruined castle overlooking the sea in Tintagel is said to be where King Arthur held court with the Knights of the Round Table; it's certainly a dramatic spot. If you're brave, you can clamber down from the ruins to the beach and explore Merlin's Cave – it's only accessible at low tide.

Don't go home without... trying to speak a few words of the native tongue: around 4,000 people still speak Kernewek, a language with strong ties to Breton and Welsh, and Cornish independence is still desired by many. Make someone's morning by greeting them with 'Myttin da'.

CLASSICALLY CORNWALL

You won't walk far here without coming across a pasty shop. The ultimate portable picnic, these pastry-encased mini-meals originally kept miners and farmers going throughout the working day. Cornish food writer Hettie Merrick has scotched the theory that they sometimes contained 'two courses', with a savoury filling at one end and a fruity one at the other. Put your disappointment aside and wrap your lips around a treat made by Hettie's daughter Ann Muller, reckoned to be Cornwall's finest pasty-maker, from the Lizard Pasty Shop in Helston (01326 290889).

DIARY

May The Daphne du Maurier Literary Festival in Fowey sees a slew of literary events, including talks, exhibitions, guided walks and concerts (www.dumaurierfestival.co.uk). June The Royal Cornwall Show, a showcase for the county's food (www.royalcornwallshow. org). August Shore things: there's the Relentless Boardmasters in Newquay's Fistral Bay (www.relentlessboardmasters.com), Falmouth Classics Regatta Week (www.falmouthweek. co.uk), and the Fowey Royal Regatta (www.foweyroyalregatta.co.uk). October Glug down bivalves at the Falmouth Oyster Festival (www.falmouthoysterfestival.co.uk).

Rosevine

←To The Beach

Driftwood

STYLE New England yacht club
SETTING Bracing Cornish clifftop

'You could hardly be closer to the sea: from our decking, the beach below is a five-minute walk through terraced gardens with hidden bothies'

I'm fairly certain that a man is not supposed to have feelings for a mackerel, especially when that very chap is sharing a weekend with his significant other at a picturesque and remote boutique hotel. But I strongly believe that we shouldn't deny our feelings, so, with apologies to Mrs Smith, I hereby confess that a mackerel fillet with celeriac and apple remoulade, beetroot and banyuls vinegar has stolen my heart. Such a shame that I had to eat it.

In case you think that these are simply the ramblings of a wistful glutton, there is a link here. The beauty of that dish was its just-caught freshness: exactly the quality that makes Driftwood, and its setting on the south Cornwall coast, so special. For those who know Cornwall's Atlantic shore – who have surfed at Newquay, or visited Jamie Oliver's Fifteen Cornwall at Watergate Bay – the south is its more modest sibling. Facing the Channel rather than the Atlantic, there are few big breakers here; the whole experience is quietly understated. The hamlet of Rosevine is almost defiantly difficult to get to (driving from the A30 takes the best part of an hour), but when you finally do arrive, you're confronted with a craggy, stark beauty.

If subtropical, sand-hemmed south Cornwall is to your taste, then there are few better ways to enjoy it than at the simple-but-stylish Driftwood hotel. You could hardly be closer to the sea: from the decking outside our room, the beach below was a five-minute walk, cutting steeply down through terraced gardens with pairs of chairs and hidden bothies for reading and thinking. It's only once you're down on the beach, maybe a hundred feet below, that you can look back up and see Driftwood as a whole. Like the landscape, it's pleasingly unostentatious: the main, extended building is a grey-blue beach house draped languidly along the hilltop that could have been shipped straight from Cape Cod. In addition, halfway down the path to the beach is 'The Cabin', a weather-boarded, family-size hidey-hole tucked into the hillside for that faux-castaway sense of seclusion.

Our room though, was up top. French windows opened onto our own terrace with sea views beyond the gardens. Like people, some hotel rooms demand to be looked at and others are more modest. Spending too much time with a show-off can be grating, so you won't find hot tubs, plasma screens or robotic toilets at Driftwood. Instead, the bedrooms are cosy, stylish and uncluttered: a battleship-sized bed takes precedence, and the ensuite is bathroom, not ballroom, sized. Lamps and mirrors are adorned with – unsurprisingly – driftwood, but that was as close as things got to frippery. Presumably, the owners reasoned that anyone wanting to cocoon themselves in a room with a DVD-library selection, when Gerrans Bay, the coastal path and the Eden Project (25 minutes away) are all close to hand, is in the wrong place anyway.

Bags unpacked, bed bounced on and free toiletries assessed (L'Occitane, since you ask), we chose the coastal path for our first excursion. From the beach, you can meander east, or west. We headed west for St Mawes, on what we thought would be a quick morning pipe-clearer. We got nowhere near, but did make it to

Portscatho, a fishing village that's home to a couple of pubs, some craft shops and Ralph's Local Stores' cluster-bomb pasties. Back at the hotel, we sat out on the decking and gorged on our meat-packed fishermen's fare.

Our mistake was not to have looked at the dinner menu before we did so, because Driftwood's restaurant is as dramatic as its setting, and head chef Chris Eden's menu is a set three courses (or seven diet-destroying broadsides if you go for the euphemistically titled 'tasting' option). The dining room overlooks the garden and has views out to sea – but we barely noticed. Our eyes were focused solely on the delights laid before us: monkfish, pollack, john dory and roasted Terras Farm duck, offset with thimble-fulls of frothy amuse-bouches and a cheese board that practically insisted we order a couple more glasses of wine to do it justice. It was impeccable, high-end cuisine, served by knowledgeable, unpretentious staff. The food and service all reflected Driftwood's appeal – high-quality local fare delivered with minimum fuss. The fact that residents are advised to book tables suggests that Driftwood is a fine-dining destination in its own right, but be warned: we'd booked a massage for the next day, but when it came to tempering the effects of Driftwood's temptations, we'd have been better off with liposuction.

Breakfast revealed our fellow guests to be a pair of families (kids are catered for with ease), some couples, and Buffy, the owners' Lakeland Terrier – who was soon shooed out. And then, a drive to a fine pub (the Kings Head in Ruan Lanihorne) for lunch, before returning for a cat-nap and a read. Some people turn to chakra-balancing, hot-stone rub-downs or reiki for their relaxation. We discovered that slumping in steamer chairs looking out over the sea, with the sun slipping away behind the promontory, does it for us. If only my sweet, succulent mackerel could have been there to enjoy it with me.

Review by Benji Wilson

'Rosevine is almost defiantly difficult to get to, but when you finally do arrive, you're confronted with a craggy, stark beauty'

NEED TO KNOW

Rooms 14 rooms, and a private cabin overlooking the beach.

Rates £165–£255, including breakfast, newspaper and, in low season, dinner. A minimum two-night stay is required at weekends; three nights on bank holidays.

Check-out 11am (but flexible); earliest check-in, 2pm.

Facilities Private beach, terrace, seven acres of heritage coastline, TV room with DVD/video library, WiFi, parking. In rooms, DVD/video player, free broadband internet access, L'Occitane toiletries.

Children Warmly welcomed. There is a £15 charge for under-12s sharing their parents' room (£20 for over-12s), including breakfast. The games room has, among other amusements, a PlayStation.

Also The kitchen will provide a picnic hamper on request. In-room beauty treatments can be booked if you need some TLC. Driftwood is closed for eight weeks in winter, usually from early December to early February.

IN THE KNOW

Our favourite rooms The Cabin has two bedrooms and its own living room, and offers perfect seclusion. The four new rooms feature six-foot beds and decked terraces, and can be connected for family groups.

Hotel bar There's a wee little bar next to the restaurant, serving all the usual tipples till midnight, but you could also take a glass of chilled wine onto the deck or the lawn and soak in that gorgeous view from a comfortable steamer chair.

Hotel restaurant Chef Chris Eden was formerly at the Square, and uses fresh, local and organic ingredients when available to produce his Modern European menu; highlights include wonderful fish and seafood and home-made bread. Last orders, 9.30pm. Breakfast heartily from 8am until 9.30am (10am on Sundays).

Top table A corner table in the new extension, or table 6 in the conservatory, overlooking the sea.

Room service Drinks and snacks only.

Dress code Chino chic: deck shoes, panama hats and cable knits.

Local knowledge Make a boat trip to the National Maritime Museum in Falmouth (www.nmmc.co.uk) – the journey itself is worthwhile; the foot-passenger ferry from St Mawes' fishing harbour leaves three times an hour, 9am–5pm, in summer, and once every hour in winter.

LOCAL EATING AND DRINKING

Tucked away in the hamlet of Ruan Lanihorne, The Kings Head (01872 501263) is a proper, good old-fashioned country pub: get there before 2pm for the perfect ploughman's or a hearty lunch of locally caught fish or pheasant (mind the shot!). Another seafood specialist, the wonderful restaurant and bar at Olga Polizzi-designed Hotel Tresanton (01326 270055) has romantic views from the terrace over the bay of St Mawes. In the fishing village of Portscatho on the Roseland peninsula, 17th-century pub The Plume of Feathers (01872 580321) is ideal for fish 'n' chips and a pint after a walk along the cliffs, or a cosy evening drink.

GET A ROOM!

For more information, or to book this hotel, go to www.mrandmrssmith.com. Register your Smith membership card (see pages 4–5) to enjoy exclusive offers and privileges.

 SMITH MEMBER OFFER　A bottle of house wine.

Driftwood Rosevine, near Portscatho, Cornwall TR2 5EW (01872 580644; www.driftwoodhotel.co.uk)

THE COTSWOLDS

COUNTRYSIDE Hillsides and honey-coloured hamlets
COUNTRY LIFE Gently does it

More typically English than a bowler-hatted Bertie Wooster whistling Elgar, this chunk of gently undulating and seemingly evergreen countryside is enough to send Anglophile tourists into apoplexy. Britain's largest designated area of natural beauty, the Cotswolds covers an area roughly bounded by Oxford to the east, Cheltenham to the west, Stratford to the north and Bath to the south. Long before the tourist invasion, the Romans left their legacy in towns such as Cirencester, and remains of villas and forts can be seen from Bury Hill to Woodchester. Today, besides sheep, the area is home to some of the country's most scenic towns and villages – all thatched cottages, ducks waddling across village greens and honey-hued churches. Other sensory delights include strolls on the beautiful banks of the River Wye, or following Fosse Way, the arrow-straight Roman road that still pierces through the loveliest landscapes imaginable.

GETTING THERE

Planes Airports closest to the region are Bristol, where easyJet (www.easyjet.com) flies from Belfast, Edinburgh, Glasgow, Inverness and Newcastle; and Birmingham, which has connections from Aberdeen, Belfast, Edinburgh, Glasgow and Jersey with BMI Baby (www.bmibaby.com).
Trains Direct trains from London Paddington run regularly to Cotswold stations, including Chippenham, Kemble, Kingham, Moreton-in-Marsh, Stroud, Gloucester and Cheltenham. Most journeys will only take an hour or two.
Automobiles From London, the Cotswolds is a couple of hours away along the M4; the nearby M5 offers access from Bristol and Birmingham. It's worth taking a car to the region: the country-lane driving is unparalleled.

LOCAL KNOWLEDGE

Taxis The smaller towns have limited taxi services – book in advance. Hotel staff will know the best local firms.
Packing tips Take a packet of Rennie if you intend to gorge on the region's renowned cheeses; and some decent walking boots and a waterproof jacket will serve you well if you plan to do any exploring on foot.

Recommended reads *Cider With Rosie*, Laurie Lee's childhood recollections of rural Gloucestershire, is perhaps the most lyrical literary evocation of the area. Jerome K Jerome's protagonists in his masterpiece of Victorian wit, *Three Men in a Boat*, drift through the Cotswolds on part of their journey. Local poet UA Fanthorpe also writes about the region – try her erudite *Collected Poems*.
Local specialities It would be perverse to come to the Cotswolds and not fill yourself with delicious Double Gloucester, a smooth whole-milk cheese first produced in the 16th century. The best is made by octogenarian Diana Smart of Old Ley Court in Churcham, who uses milk from her herd of Brown Swiss, Holstein and Gloucester cows (www.smartsgloucestercheese.com).
Perfect picnic Bourton-on-the-Water, just a few miles from Stow-on-the-Wold, is an idyllic English village where trees dreamily dip their branches into the River Windrush as dragonflies skim its surface. Laze the afternoon away on the riverbank with filled baguettes (cheese and pickle, prawns in seafood sauce, or lamb and mayo) from Norah's Pantry (01451 820815).

And... Before railway timetables were first drawn up in the mid-19th century, villagers in Stroud set their time by the sun. Being some 90 miles west of the meridian, noon was nine minutes later than in Greenwich. Some locals are still campaigning to bring back what was known as Stroud Time.

WORTH GETTING OUT OF BED FOR

Viewpoint Just north of Stow-on-the-Wold, the Broadway Tower is a glorious folly, built like a mock castle and perched 312 metres above sea level, offering soul-soothing views across the Severn Valley to the Welsh mountains.

Arts and culture The Arts and Crafts design movement began in this area in the 19th century, and its influence is everywhere: Kelmscott Manor, the house William Morris shared with Dante Gabriel Rossetti, is well worth a visit (www.kelmscottmanor.co.uk). There are more Arts and Crafts wonders at Rodmarton Manor in Cirencester (01285 841253) and Hidcote Manor Garden, near Chipping Campden (01386 438333). The Cheltenham Festival of Literature (www.cheltenhamfestivals.com), held every October, is attended by eminent writers such as Stephen Fry, Maya Angelou and Bret Easton Ellis.

Activities A favourite with Princes Charles, William and Harry, Beaufort Polo Club near Tetbury is one of the finest places in the country to take in a chukka or two (www.beaufortpoloclub.co.uk). Up the horsepower at Castle Combe, a racing circuit where you can take a selection of seriously fast cars for a spin – or keep it simple and go go-karting (www.castlecombecircuit.co.uk). For a flying lesson or trip in a microlight, contact Kemble Flying Club near Cirencester (01285 770077; www.kembleflyingclub.co.uk). Taking it down many more notches, haven't you always wanted to try dry-stone walling? Volunteer to repair dry-stone walls or partake in altruistic hedgelaying and tree planting from bases in Cheltenham and Gloucester (www.gvcv.org.uk).

Daytripper Possibly the most tranquil attraction in the sleepy Cotswolds, the national arboretum at Westonbirt (www.forestry.gov.uk/westonbirt) has one of the world's most spectacular tree collections. You can happily spend a day kicking up leaves and gazing at the neck-crickingly tall redwoods. Take a picnic – and binoculars.

Children Kids love Romans almost as much as they love dinosaurs. Take them to Cirencester where, on your command, they can poke around the ruins pretending they're centurions. Then it's on to the town's revamped Corinium Museum, which offers a range of child-friendly, Roman-centric activities (www.coriniummuseum.co.uk).

Walks Walking in this neck of the woods is a joy. Pick a section of the 105-mile Cotswold Way. Alternatively, the South Cotswold Ramblers website offers an exhaustive list of tantalising trails in Gloucester and other towns in the region (www.southcotswoldramblers.org.uk).

Shopping Stow-on-the-Wold is the epicentre for antiques – but equally worthwhile is a pokeabout in the dusty shops of Burford, Cirencester, Moreton-in-Marsh and Tetbury. Cotswold markets are invariably rewarding: head for Moreton-in-Marsh on Tuesdays, Tetbury on Wednesdays, and Cirencester on Mondays and Fridays. Foodies can also spend many happy hours in Tetbury's House of Cheese (www.houseofcheese.co.uk), home to a life-affirmingly wonderful selection of fromage, as well as chutneys and pickles; and pick up mouthwatering luxuries at the pre-eminent Daylesford Organic Farm Shop, which also has an excellent café and an indulgent homewares shop (www.daylesfordorganic.com).

Something for nothing Bliss out for free at the fabulous Rococo Garden at Painswick (www.rococogarden.org.uk), which was completely overgrown until the 1970s. Now restored, it's a wonderful place in which to surround yourself with birdsong and bee buzz.

Don't go home without... buying a bottle of easy-drinking English white from the Three Choirs Vineyards in Newent (01531 890223). Team it with Double Gloucester at your next Seventies-themed cheese-and-wine party.

CONCLUSIVELY COTSWOLDS

The area's famously photogenic hamlets and villages owe much of their attractiveness to Cotswold stone, a yellow limestone quarried in the region's eponymous hills. The hue changes depending on the source: Northern Cotswold stone is characterised by a rich, honeyed gold; as you approach Bath, the colour is a delicate pale buttermilk.

DIARY

March The Cheltenham Festival horse-racing fixture culminates in the famous Gold Cup (www.cheltenham.co.uk). **May** Cheltenham Jazz Festival (www.cheltenhamfestivals.com) brings in big musical names for goateed men to nod along to. **May/June** Until 2010 Cooper's Hill in Gloucestershire hosted a cheese-rolling competition, but health and safety may have put paid to this annual event where people hurtle themselves downhill after an eight-pound 'squircle' of Double Gloucester. Boo. **August** If it's flared nostrils and shimmering fetlocks you're after, head to the Festival of British Eventing at Gatcombe Park (www.gatcombe-horse. co.uk) for daredevil displays of dressage, showjumping and cross-country riding. **September** Find a tuffet to sit on and enjoy the curds and whey at Cheltenham's Great British Cheese Festival and British Cheese Awards (0845 241 2026). Tastings, workshops and cheese tossing!

Barnsley House

STYLE Super-stylish manor house
SETTING Gorgeous Gloucestershire gardens

'A beguiling collision of the landscaped and the wild, the grounds of Barnsley House are the stuff of period-drama fantasy'

I sail boats, and I live by the sea in Brighton. In fact, when I'm reborn, I'd like (karma willing) to come back as a pirate. With that in mind, you'll understand that when I'm not living and breathing the buccaneer's life, I'm probably dreaming about it. So imagine my bewilderment as, roused from my seafaring slumber, I find myself being bundled into a car – and not a boat. No cutlasses or pieces of eight here. Just three large weekend bags, two Ms Smiths, and one very bleary-eyed, hung-over would-be pirate. While I'm fighting off the waves of nausea from a stag do the night before, Mrs Smith gently reminds me of our mission: to review Barnsley House in the Cotswolds, with our four-month-old daughter Delilah. Now, if I can only stop my stomach churning like I'm about to walk the plank, we might make it there in one piece.

Although many manor houses have an unfortunate tendency to be inland, they have always seriously impressed me, and, pulling up at this 17th-century skyline-loomer, I'm not disappointed. By the time we've disembarked at the ivy-hugged, hilltop mansion, I've completely recovered my land legs. There's something about the aged Cotswold stone and manicured setting that sends me back to childhood summers at my grandmother's Ireland home, and it takes the sultry French tones of a Barnsley House staff member to pull me out of my nostalgic reverie. Dispensing with the formality of check-in, she guides us straight to our room. We're in the new Stable Yard, with a split-level suite. The ground floor consists of a marshmallow-comfy double bed and a sleek, spacious lounge area with windows overlooking the courtyard.

Now is the moment of truth. Mrs Smith is a fashion stylist and has a laser-guided eye for the tiniest design flaws. As she conducts her silent survey, I await the inevitable 'tsk' that greets even the most invisible aesthetic faux pas. But, miraculously, none comes. I sigh with relief, and a smiling Mrs Smith disappears up the wrought-iron staircase into the crow's nest of our suite – a bathroom on a floor all of its own. Running up to join her, I find a glass wall that gives a perfect view of our bedroom below. A claw-foot roll-top bath presides over the space, partnered by a freestanding shower with a frying-pan-sized head, a TV set into the wall and a soapstone basin almost a metre in length.

The courtyard below boasts a waterfall surrounded by a medley of meadow flowers: pansies, foxgloves and heather – but it's the beautiful main gardens that have caught our eye. So, having transferred Delilah from armchair to pushchair, we set off for the formal lawns. A beguiling collision of the landscaped and the wild, the grounds of Barnsley House are the stuff of period-drama fantasy. Shaded paths weave around hidden statues, curvaceous topiary and bountiful berry bushes. We find ourselves resting in an ivy-draped gazebo, looking out onto a lily-capped carp pond. We can see why horticulturalites from around the world head to this garden of delights (although presumably they don't get presented with delicious apple martinis by a passing barman while they're inspecting the cabbages).

Arriving at seven o'clock on the dot, the hotel's babysitter enables us to enjoy an aperitif before dinner. Sinking into my seat I order monkfish tempura with Barnsley House-grown vegetables. Mrs Smith announces she is not hungry – a claim belied a few minutes later when most of my monkfish has fallen victim to her scavenging fork. I order another, then top it with a delectable helping of fresh strawberries, rich cream and crumbly shortbread. Happy, we saunter to our enormous bed (post-nightcap, of course), tuck the snoozing little one between us, and sleep the sleep of the fabulously stuffed.

After waking to a leisurely 11 o'clock breakfast in bed (muesli, yoghurt, jams and croissants), we're tempted to linger longer in the linens, but also determined to squeeze every last drop of grade II-listed glamour from this hotel. We take the path to the spa building – all glass and Cotswold stone – under the shadow of the neighbouring farm. There's a steam room and sauna (as well as bowls of crushed ice on hand for the necessary post-steaming facial cool-down) and a massage menu that's relaxing just to read, but it's the heated outdoor hydrotherapy pool that really gets me excited. Then I realise I've forgotten my swimming shorts (why would I need them this far inland?). Not to worry; the staff seem only mildly alarmed at the sight of a man in his boxers. Perhaps they're used to it.

Alternately wallowing and being pummelled by the giant overhead jets of water, I feel a million miles away from the hung-over pirate of yesterday. Shuffling into the relaxation room, we find ourselves reclining on black leather loungers and sipping ginger tea, against a backdrop of inimitable Cotswolds countryside spied through floor-to-ceiling glass walls; it's a drop-dead delicious denouement to our already perfect day.

It's tempting to skip dinner, but sister inn, the Village Pub across the road, has a reputation not to be resisted. We're provided with a spot-on wine recommendation to suit our gourmet pub supper, and the head gardener, regales us with a lesson in veg-growing that reminds me that sometimes the land does have its advantages over the ocean – after all, you can't grow cauliflower on a catamaran.

We're scheduled to leave Barnsley House tomorrow morning, and normally I'm straining at the moorings to get back to my beloved marina, but – shiver me oak-beamed timbers – I never thought I'd be this reluctant to return to the sea.

Reviewed by Jim McNulty

NEED TO KNOW

Rooms 18, including 11 suites.

Rates £275–£545, including English breakfast.

Check-out Midday (5pm check-out available on payment of a £75 supplement). Check-in, 3pm.

Facilities Landscaped gardens, tennis court, helipad, holistic spa with hydrotherapy pool, private 30-seat cinema, DVD library. In rooms, plasma-screen TV with surround-sound system, CD/DVD player, iPod dock, free broadband connection, mini fridge with complimentary water and juice. Fresh fruit and tea and coffee also available. Bikes to borrow.

Children Extra beds (£45) or cots (£20) can be provided. Babysitting can be arranged (£10 an hour). A children's menu is available in the restaurant, too.

Also There are occasionally afternoon or evening film screenings; you can also hire the cinema, from £200 for three hours.

IN THE KNOW

Our favourite rooms Bathrooms are a big draw here, with features such as roll-top baths, twin sinks, walk-through showers and flatscreen TVs. Room 1 has two bathtubs, side by side; Room 2 has a Jacuzzi. Room 8 has a sitting room, and Room 7 has its own conservatory and garden. Stableyard Rooms are attractive duplexes with upstairs bathrooms and wet rooms.

Hotel bar The cosy country-style bar is warm, woody and willowy, and is open until late for guests.

Hotel restaurant The secret of the Potager's super-fresh Modern European dishes is home-grown vegetables, salad leaves and herbs plucked straight from the kitchen garden (when you see zucchini soup and deep-fried courgette flowers on the same menu, it's easy to tell what's ripe for the picking). Breakfast, 7.30am–10.30am (noon for room service).

Top table Table 4, in the bay window.

Room service Food can be ordered while the kitchen is open (8am–10pm); they may be able to rustle up snacks out of hours.

Dress code Relaxed but stylish; leave ripped jeans and elderly T-shirts at home.

Local knowledge Grab a pair of gumboots and a walking map from reception and explore the countryside (if you're really keen, ring ahead and reserve wellies in your size). Staff can also arrange fantastic activities from rowing along the Thames with a picnic hamper to side-saddle riding lessons.

LOCAL EATING AND DRINKING

With polished-wood tables, crackling fires and exposed beams, **The Village Pub** (01285 740421), across the road from Barnsley House, is not only a wonderful place to nurse a pint (or a Pimm's), but also does fantastic food. **Jesse's Bistro** in Cirencester (01285 641497) is a small, relaxed restaurant with its own cheese shop, serving fresh fish and meat roasted in a wood-burning oven. You'll find it in a stableyard behind the highly regarded butcher's, Jesse Smiths. Just outside Cirencester in Ewen, 16th-century **Wild Duck Inn** (01285 770310) is a step-back-in-time treat, with oak panelling, an enormous fireplace and ancestral oil paintings. It's a lovely place for a few drinks; there's real ale on tap and a killer wine list, but the big draw is the canopied courtyard with an ancient apple tree at its, ahem, core. On Tetbury's Cirencester Road in a converted jail, **Trouble House Inn** (01666 502206) is an option for country-pub grub. Another good dining option is **The Bell at Sapperton** (01285 760298), where most ingredients of its gastropub menu are locally sourced.

GET A ROOM!

For more information, or to book this hotel, go to www.mrandmrssmith.com. Register your Smith membership card (see pages 4–5) to enjoy exclusive offers and privileges.

SMITH MEMBER OFFER A Barnsley House champagne cocktail each – or a glass of champagne in the Village Pub across the road – on each night of your stay.

Barnsley House Barnsley, Cirencester, Gloucestershire GL7 5EE (01285 740000; www.barnsleyhouse.com)

Cotswold House

STYLE State-of-the-art comfort zone
SETTING Charming Chipping Campden

'I distract her with suite talk: palatial bath, disco shower, private courtyard, three TVs, a remote-control fire...'

Mrs Smith is AWOL. Her Gloucestershire-bound train from Paddington has been delayed. As a result, I'm alone in Cotswold House's sleek Sezincote suite, watching a Chinese vet giving a panda what one might refer to as an 'executive massage'. Sir David Attenborough's soothing toffee tones fill the snug, fire-warmed lounge; as I crack open a minibar merlot, the giant TV tells me about panda porn, animal Viagra and breeding these black-and-white bears in captivity.

Perhaps it's the wine, or maybe I'm missing my lady, but when cubs finally appear on the scene – bald, blind and mewling like kittens – I shed a (manly) tear. It's moving stuff, this mating lark so I decide to explore a Christmas fair outside. It's bitingly cold, and only the hardiest are out, scarf-wrapped and hat-topped. All I can spy of the locals are a chink of eyes here, a glint of teeth there – they might be aliens beneath their thermals. However, Chipping Campden is too pretty for sci-fi thoughts, so instead I shop for beauty unguents for my sweetheart.

As a second free mince pie makes it into my mouth, Mrs Smith rings to announce her arrival. I hasten back to our stately Regency townhouse, to find her waiting by a crackling fire in reception. Another hearth in full flame can be heard nearby in the bar – if there were an award for 'Hotel with the Most Most-Crackling Fires', Cotswold House would win. As Mrs Smith tries to pry in my bags, I distract her with suite talk: 'Palatial bath, disco shower, private courtyard, three TVs, a remote-control fire...'

My spiel works; by the time I'm mentioning the Temple Spa products, Mrs Smith is flinging open Sezincote's door to discover the boutique bounty for herself. I trail around in her wake, offering bits of trivia – 'The shower's LED lights change colour, the spa can be accessed from our courtyard, I ordered you an orthopaedic pillow' – until Mrs Smith silences me by diving onto our bed, heels and all. All that animal mating earlier might have spurred me on to strip my Mrs Smith, but there's an obstacle: I'm hungry. Starving, in fact. Mrs Smith is in accord; we de-rumple our attire and head to the restaurant. Ruby-red Hicks' is a hotel hug: warm and inviting, relaxed but luxurious, smart without being stuffy.

Nestled in a fireside nook, Mrs Smith and I study the menu. One glance and I'm happy – it's short but beguiling; of the seven or so mains, I'm torn between five. We embark on a waistline-widening feast: roast pheasant and a silky quail's egg, duck so tender it must have lived off butter and marshmallows, an earthy pumpkin salad, a ravishing apricot soufflé, and a cheeseboard in a rainbow of local varieties. Such excess is exhausting – when Mrs Smith and I retire, we clamber into bed and promptly start snoring.

The next morning, I awake and leap straight to my feet. Having arrived in darkness, neither of us has properly appraised our surroundings. I yank the curtains aside, realise I'm still naked, scream like a girl, and dive back into bed. Mrs Smith, in contrast, stands serenely in her robe and admires our courtyard. 'There's nobody to see you', she reminds me. 'And if they could, who's to say they'd be interested?' she laughs.

A bath is begging to be run in the gargantuan stone cauldron lording it over our ensuite, and soon Mrs Smith is asoaking, emerging only to peep at the TV flickering on the wall. Meanwhile, I marvel at the raspberry and emerald lights in the shower – where I'd stay all morning, if Mrs Smith's stomach didn't start rumbling. Breakfast is most civilised: we sit in the Garden Room by the French windows, perusing the papers. Mrs Smith tackles whisky-laced porridge, before we both demolish a faultless full English.

From one pleasure to another; it's Temple Spa time. Having crunched along the garden path, admiring the manicured hedges and sculptures, Mrs Smith then commandeers the pool, before hitting the hammam. I'm dispatched to a massage room and treated like human pastry: pummelled, kneaded and flattened. Not a fan of the timorous poke-and-stroke variety, I'm putty in masseuse Melissa's forceful hands. Ingeniously, my massage bed is heated, and I slip into an impromptu slumber. 'You fell asleep,' murmurs my therapist as I come to. 'Oh no – I wasn't snoring?' I ask. 'No,' she replies. 'But you were sleeptalking. And I could swear you mumbled something about pandas and Viagra.'

Reviewed by Chomoi Picho-Owiny

'I'm putty in my masseuse's hands and I slip into an impromptu slumber'

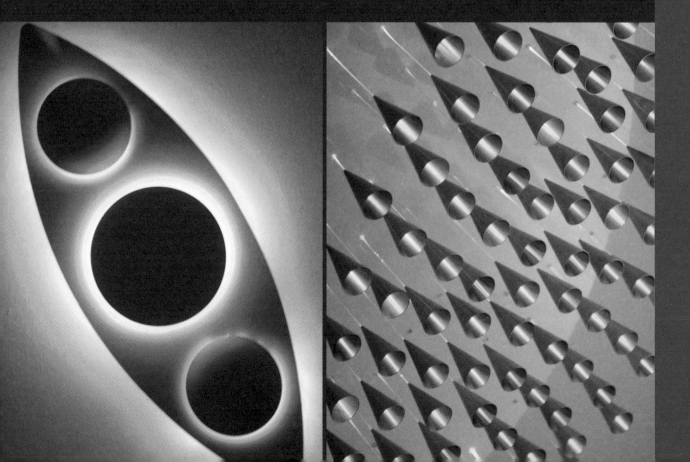

NEED TO KNOW

Rooms 28, including three suites.

Rates £170–£500, including breakfast.

Check-out 11.30am.

Facilities Spa with hammam and hydrotherapy pool, gardens, croquet lawn, DVD/CD library, pillow and bedding menu. In rooms, flatscreen TV (some in the bathrooms), CD/DVD player, minibar, tea/coffee, free broadband internet access.

Children Cotswold House is family-friendly: there is a children's menu, and cots and high chairs are free to borrow. Foldaway beds can be provided for £35 a night.

Also Dogs can be accommodated; ring ahead for details. You can also pre-order supplies for your minibar, specify how you'd like the bed made up, and request which Temple Spa toiletries you'd like supplied in the bathroom.

IN THE KNOW

Our favourite rooms All the cottage rooms are lovely; ask for one with its own fireplace. Hidcote Cottage and Longborough Suite have private gardens with outdoor hot tubs. Rooms in the Montrose House wing are all-singing and all-dancing, with in-shower mood lighting and bath tubs built for two: room 11 has a steam bath; the Sezincote suite has a stone bath.

Hotel bar The Pavilion Bar serves drinks and light meals on the terrace in good summer weather. Juliana's Bar is open as long as residents are cosied up on its inviting sofas. Delicious champagne cocktails are served in Hicks' bar.

Hotel restaurant Hicks' champions local ingredients, with the occasional Continental influence, for example: bream with saffron and mussel bouillon. Breakfast is served in the airy Garden Room.

Top table Dine outside, weather permitting; inside, near the French windows.

Room service There's a full menu until the kitchens close at 9.30pm (10pm at weekends) and cold snacks thereafter.

Dress code Things are nicely relaxed here, but you may want to snazz up a little for dinner.

Local knowledge Cotswold House can organise all manner of diverting activities, from quad biking and clay-pigeon shooting to trout fishing. Cirencester Park Polo Club – the UK's oldest – is set in gorgeous grounds; rock up on a Sunday and have a picnic while you watch a couple of chukkas, followed by a few sundowners at the bar (www.cirencesterpolo.co.uk).

LOCAL EATING AND DRINKING

In the centre of the village, **Eight Bells** (01386 840371) is a traditional pub that's ideal for a Sunday roast after a long walk, or a casual supper. You'll need to book, unless you're lucky enough to get an alfresco table on the terrace. Also on the Square, **The Kings'** restaurant (01386 840256) is brimming with country charm and cheer, and has a 'greatest hits' menu of Brit classics with an experimental streak: try steak and kidney sausages with bubble and squeak. A 10-minute drive away in Shipston on Stour, **The George** (01608 661453) has a relaxed bar with all-day eating options, as well as a more refined dining room. If you crave all-out luxury, hot-foot it to Cheltenham, where, as well as culinary heavyweight **Le Champignon Sauvage** (01242 573449) and upscale **Lumière** (01242 222200), there's **The Daffodil** (01242 700055), elegantly housed in a converted art deco cinema. Expect a neat line in mouthwateringly modern Anglo-Mediterranean dishes. **The Noel Arms Hotel** (01386 840317) is Cotswold House's sister property (it's just across the street), and here you will find a smart restaurant and a snug bar.

GET A ROOM!

For more information, or to book this hotel, go to www.mrandmrssmith.com. Register your Smith membership card (see pages 4–5) to enjoy exclusive offers and privileges.

 SMITH MEMBER OFFER Choose between afternoon tea for two and a bottle of champagne.

Cotswold House The Square, Chipping Campden, Gloucestershire GL55 6AN (01386 840330; www.cotswoldhouse.com)

Lower Slaughter Manor

STYLE Refined country seat
SETTING Gloucestershire's prettiest village

'Luxe drapery in opulent fabrics: yup.
Sexy aubergine and taupe colour scheme:
check. Princess-and-the-Pea-dimensioned
bed: can't miss it'

I had my first afternoon at Lower Slaughter Manor all worked out: we'd arrive, explore, potter, drink tea – and then I'd let the pampering commence. Except, my in-room facial and pedicure was supposed to start half an hour ago, and we were still stuck in a tailback in the wrong county, with temperatures rising and blood boiling. When we'd set off from home, it had been the kind of glorious, early summer day on which, if you're not careful, you burn your driving arm on the sunny side. Mr Smith scalded his. 'Lower Slaughter' – a name that was already proving strangely apt, thanks to the en-route limb reddening.

A hint of Hammer House isn't an obvious element in the name of a boutique getaway. But thankfully, images of horror-movie carnage are the last thing to spring to mind as you crunch up the 18th-century coach house's

sweeping gravel drive. The imposing country manor, which overlooks a gentle curve in the dreamy River Eye, has got that tranquillity thing down to a T, with its bowling-green perfect lawn, ancestral chestnut and beech trees, and walled gardens dotted with statues, old climbing roses and gnarly fruit trees.

I don't know why I'd got so hot and bothered about being late; nobody else was. Check-in is a seamless affair and Mr Smith barely gets a chance to dump his suitcase in our room before he's banished with his book to make way for the therapist who has managed to rearrange her schedule so she can make my pain go away. A few calming moments later, the garden doors are open, and I'm zoning out with a lavender-and-mint-scented zephyr wafting over me from the walled garden outside. The only thing that breaks my trance is a low, rhythmic grunting sound. Which – *quelle horreur* – I realise is me. Snoring.

Still, I'm in the perfect position to check out the decor. This is classic country-house chic, but with enough contemporary flourishes to knock any suggestion of fuddy-duddiness on the head. I mentally tick off my list of requirements: luxe drapery in opulent fabrics: yup. Sexy aubergine and taupe colour scheme: check. Enormous, Princess-and-the-Pea-dimensioned bed: can't miss it. Knock-out bathroom? I think the freestanding claw-foot bath and the wet room have got that covered. All that, *and* an abundance of scatter cushions. You get the feeling that if you were to fall, you'd never be too far from something soft and squishy to bounce you back up again. Oh yes, I'm feeling to the manor born and, on discovering the complimentary decanter of sherry, come over all Penelope Keith. Mr Smith, on the other hand, is busy eyeing up the enormous flatscreen plasma TV, the free WiFi and iPod-ready stereo. Men really are from Mars.

But the best was yet to come. I don't know how we missed it but, tucked inside our private, walled garden is a huge hot tub, complete with sparkly lights for added LA-style glamour. It's a shame I hadn't known it was there, otherwise I'd have brought my bikini. (Well, a shame for anyone in the room upstairs that happens to glance down upon us as I dive in, *sans swimwear*.)

All pampered and hot-tubbed, I'm sorely in need of a pre-dinner reviver. With no main bar, drinks are served in lounges, all stuffed full with antique furniture, gilt-framed paintings and dominated by enormous log fireplaces. It feels like we've wandered, unchallenged, into a gentleman's club in Piccadilly – only without the cigar smoke and old boys.

We sip our aperitifs and pore over the dinner menu which, as well as your old-school favourites (smoked salmon, Châteaubriand, tarte tatin), also has your contemporary classics (Gloucestershire Old Spot, line-caught sea bass). Appetites suitably whetted, we head through to the chocolate-brown dining room, where hushed conversations are punctuated by the chink of crystal goblet and the scrape of chunky silver on fine bone china. It's the kind of experience that would make any girl feel special.

Breakfast is served in the same room. But, come morning, we discover that the daylight has transformed Lower Slaughter's dining room into an airy, sunny space with engaging views of the gardens, which are a perfect blend of formal and cottage planting.

I'd love to report that we worked off the calories of our full English breakfasts by getting up at dawn for a canter across dewy fields, before fitting in a round of golf at the local 18-hole course. We do at least talk about a spot of tennis. But then we get held up pootling about in Chipping Norton, where we end up eating slabs of home-made chocolate cake and people-watching outside the charming, independent Jaffe and Neale bookshop and café. The combination of sedate pace, country air and obscene amounts of carbohydrate has rendered us good for not much other than sighing happily and eating more cake.

We meander back through the kind of green and pleasant picture-perfect scenes that calendar salesmen make fortunes from. Enamoured of the country life, I even sneak a look in a few local estate agents' windows and innocently mention to self-confessed, die-hard townie Mr Smith that, if the Young Farmers need any (not-so-young) recruits, I'd like to be considered. If it hadn't been such an incredibly romantic escape, I think my comment might have earned me the kind of reaction that would make Lower Slaughter live up to its name after all...

Reviewed by Mr & Mrs Smith

'It feels like we've wandered, unchallenged, into a gentleman's club in Piccadilly – only without the cigar smoke and old boys'

NEED TO KNOW

Rooms 19, including nine suites.

Rates £310–£850, including tea/coffee, newspaper, and full English breakfast.

Check-out 11am, but flexible subject to availability. Check-in, 2pm.

Facilities Five acres of landscaped gardens, croquet lawn, tennis court, DVD library. In rooms, Vi-Spring mattresses, TV, CD/DVD player, iPod dock, free WiFi, bottled water and sherry, fresh fruit, L'Occitane toiletries.

Children Three sets of rooms can be connected for families. Cots (£15) and extra beds (£75 a night) can be provided.

Also Book in-room beauty treatments, or get the hotel to arrange boredom-busting activities: they can sort out anything from archery and rock-climbing to murder-mystery evenings, blind 4x4 driving, and duck herding. Yes, you did read that correctly.

IN THE KNOW

Our favourite rooms For an extravagant weekend of romance, book one of the ground-floor Garden rooms in the Coach House: Valentine Strong is a decadent suite with a bathroom featuring twin roll-top baths that gives onto a private garden with a hot tub; Magnolia is a huge double with a freestanding bath and private garden. Deluxe and Master rooms on the second floor of the main house have wonderful views of the village; Mrs Smiths will love Longborough – it has a freestanding roll-top bath and a separate dressing room.

Hotel bar There's no bar, but waiters will bring you whatever you desire. The drinks menu will melt whisky-lovers' hearts.

Hotel restaurant Silk-lined, crystal-spangled Sixteen58 offers fine dining from Stuart Ralston using local, seasonal delights. The sommelier has amassed an impressive cellar of vintage champagnes and prestige wines.

Top table An intimate table for two overlooking the gardens.

Room service During restaurant hours you can order from the Sixteen58 menu, out of those hours classic room service favourites are available, such as grilled sandwiches and soup.

Dress code It's not stuffy here, but pack your smartest casuals.

Local knowledge The Georgian charms of Cheltenham are a few miles' drive away. Have a nose around town, or attend an event at one of the festivals: there's jazz in May, a series of science events in June, music in July and literature in October (www.cheltenhamfestivals.co.uk).

LOCAL EATING AND DRINKING

Set in a honey-coloured rectory in Upper Slaughter, the whisper-quiet, romantic restaurant at Lords of the Manor is known for its on-trend British cuisine (01451 820243). At the Royalist Hotel in Stow-on-the-Wold, 947AD (01451 830670) has a menu that reads like a mediaeval banquet of meat, fish and game, including ox cheeks, mackerel and guinea fowl. Next door, its gastropub Eagle and Child (01451 830670) is a popular lunchtime stop-off, serving British favourites cooked with flair – we love the steak, kidney and thyme suet pudding. Booking is advisable at both on busy weekends. In Chipping Campden, have a pre-dinner cocktail at the bar in Hicks' Brasserie at Cotswold House, before moving into Juliana's Restaurant to enjoy its excellent Modern British and Mediterranean menu (01386 840330).

GET A ROOM!

For more information, or to book this hotel, go to www.mrandmrssmith.com. Register your Smith membership card (see pages 4–5) to enjoy exclusive offers and privileges.

 SMITH MEMBER OFFER A bottle of champagne in your room, and late check-out (subject to availability).

Lower Slaughter Manor **Lower Slaughter, Gloucestershire GL54 2HP** (01451 820456; www.lowerslaughter.co.uk)

Crudwell

Rectory Hotel

STYLE Period-detail family retreat
SETTING Walled gardens in Wiltshire

'With its open log fires, canoodle-friendly armchairs and all that crisp Egyptian linen waiting for you upstairs, it's the perfect place to kickstart or rekindle a romance'

under-sevens in tow, all that peace and quiet is a worry. I needn't have fretted. While there's none of the hubbub that comes as standard with 'family-focused' hotels, Mr Smith and I are pleased to report that this is an adult-friendly place to stay that caters for kids on the no-pressure understanding that they'll behave.

Set in three acres of walled gardens, this 17th-century Cotswold-stone house started life as the rectory for the Saxon church next door. Its new owners, Jonathan (ex-Hotel du Vin) and Julian (an antiques/art dealer and interior designer) have given it a makeover that's considerate of the architecture, yet has enough contemporary twists to make us feel at home, rather than trapped in a heritage piece.

Wood panelling and hand-sprung mattresses, cream walls and muted plaid-and-floral fabrics – period detail with sufficient modern accents to assure its boutique-hotel status. While there is mobile-phone coverage and a computer available for guests to use, you'll probably get more use out of the cricket bats and croquet sets piled up by the front door. I know we did.

I head for our roomy, tastefully furnished pale-palette suite to unpack, where wooden beams and a fireplace combine to create a charming old-world ambience that wouldn't be out of place in a Jane Austen novel. Taking a minute to breathe in the views over the Victorian gardens, I can hear the distant sound of leather thwacking willow as Mr Smith tries vainly to share his cricketing prowess.

I slip on a robe, eschewing the temptaton of a deep bath and its accompanying Arran Aromatics for a trip to the heated outdoor pool, blissfully happy about the fact that I'll never have to understand the difference between a silly mid-off and deep gully.

It's no wonder that this property manages to attract so many courting couples. With its open log fires, canoodle-friendly armchairs and all that crisp Egyptian linen waiting for you upstairs, this is the perfect place to kickstart or rekindle a romance.

W hen escaping for the weekend, there's always a moment – usually just after the 14th 'are we there yet?' – when you wonder if this really was such a good idea. Especially when you're headed for a place called Crudwell. Things weren't looking good. With three scratchy boys fidgeting in the back and one increasingly impatient lad at the wheel, my dreams of a few restful days in the countryside were fading fast. Until we arrived at Rectory Hotel.

You could be forgiven for thinking we'd pulled up at the country pile of a very flush friend. It certainly doesn't look like a hotel. There's no reception, just a simple desk in the front room. No computers. No phone. And no fellow guests milling about. Just calm, hear-a-pin-drop silence. They say it's golden, but when you have three energetic

While Mr Smith retreads the croquet- and cricket-induced divots, I take the boys into the wood-panelled restaurant for their high tea – chef Peter Fairclough's pared-down version of what's to come later. The setting may sound formal, but the glorious garden vistas (meals can be served outside in the summer months) must make dinner the most alluring element of the hotel for most guests, and the sneak preview merely offers more incentive to get the kids bathed and bedded as soon as possible so we can have our turn come dinnertime.

Chef's a follower of the Slow Food Movement and serves up a very British menu (English asparagus, Welsh lamb, Pimm's jelly, in case you're curious) with everything locally sourced, seasonal, GM-free and organic. Mr Smith is tempted to finish off with a slice of Stinking Bishop from the nearby cheese-producing village of Dymock, which prompts no end of smutty innuendo.

The fact that as much as possible is sourced within half an hour of the hotel all sounds worthy. What is not so worthy is how Mr Smith, myself and all the little Smiths manage to devour enough produce between us to cause a Wiltshire-wide food shortage. However, we can now justifiably declare that Rectory's modern British cuisine is, in the words of the three-year-old, 'yum, yum, yummy and nice'. We retreat, replete, to a cosy corner complete with whisky and backgammon.

The following morning, we get up with the sun, on a mission to explore the area, away from all garden sports. First stop is Westonbirt Arboretum. Yes, it's just a collection of trees. And yes, you have to pay for the privilege of walking through them. But there are 3,000 different species, in every imaginable colour, many of them rare and endangered. To my surprise, before long, the six- and three-year-old are compiling a list of their favourites and are kept captivated all through the walk – so, hey, let's not knock the arboretum.

As the clouds roll in, we take cover in nearby sleepy Tetbury where I manage a crafty look round the antiques shops. Unfortunately, there's no room in the car for the coffee table that catches my eye. Mr Smith's relief is

palpable. Dawdling back to the Rectory, the rain descends, scuppering the boys' plans to spend all afternoon in the pool and Mr Smith's thoughts of taking to the Cotswold Way – a mere 100-mile trail.

I, on the other hand, make the most of the adverse weather conditions, curling up to work my way through about two dozen fashion and lifestyle magazines. As we head back to London, we can't help marvelling at how easy it is to spend so much time doing so little. And Rectory Hotel is a great place not to rush things.

Reviewed by Emma Loach

'No computers. No mobile phones...
Just calm, hear-a-pin-drop silence'

NEED TO KNOW

Rooms 12.

Rates £95–£195, including breakfast. There's a two-night minimum stay over bank holiday weekends or public holidays.

Check-out 11am (can be extended to midday in some cases). Check-in, 3pm, but flexible subject to availability.

Facilities Heated outdoor pool; gardens with croquet lawn; library of books, CDs and DVDs; free WiFi; loaner iPod and digital camera; wellies and walking maps. In rooms, flatscreen TV, CD/DVD player, iPod dock, Bamford toiletries.

Children As befits the former home of a rector who had 14 children, the hotel is very family-friendly. Cots and baby monitors are available; an extra bed costs £15 a night, including breakfast. There's a children's menu, and babysitting is £8 an hour.

Also Canine guests welcome. Book a massage, either at the hotel or at a nearby spa. Try a game of pétanque on the lawn.

IN THE KNOW

Our favourite rooms Every room has a view over the gardens; they are similarly decorated in pale, soothing colours, but all have unique details, such as a fireplace or wooden beams. Of the Deluxe rooms, we like Leckhampton for its huge bed and roll-top bath; Sudeley has a four-poster. Standard rooms Nympsfield and Cam Peak can be combined for families.

Hotel bar Smart armchairs, comfy sofas and Perspex tables strike just the right balance between homely and stylish. If G&Ts aren't your thing, there's an excellent list of wines and whiskies; the bar closes when the last guest has gone to bed.

Hotel restaurant You can't fail to enjoy Peter Fairclough's Modern British menu of fresh, seasonal produce – mostly organic – especially in summer, when it's served outside in the Victorian gardens. The restaurant comprises two spaces: a handsomely wood-panelled dining room and a bright, airy conservatory. For pub-style fare, skip to the Potting Shed.

Top table The light and the garden views are wonderful, so choose a table by the windows.

Room service A full menu is available during restaurant hours, but the kitchen can usually magic up a sandwich, salad or omelette if you're peckish at peculiar times.

Dress code Battered casuals won't do your genteel surroundings any justice, but things are very low-key here.

Local knowledge Go for a helicopter ride or aerobatic flight at Kemble airfield, or try piloting a light aircraft. Your partner can join you in the cabin if you book a one-hour trial lesson, or there are instructed return trips to the Isle of Wight (stopping for a civilised lunch). For details, contact the Flying Club Kemble (01285 771025; www.theflyingclubkemble.com).

LOCAL EATING AND DRINKING

The Potting Shed (01666 577833) is across the common right here in Crudwell, and is the sister pub to the Rectory; here you can enjoy an exuberantly British menu of seasonal produce such as honey-glazed roast rabbit in Farrow & Ball'd surroundings. Nearby in Tetbury, Calcot Manor (01666 890391) has two restaurants: book dinner for truly fine dining in The Conservatory, or drop in on its gastropub The Gumstool Inn on your way home from Westonbirt Arboretum. Adjacent to Malmesbury's abbey, wisteria-covered 13th-century inn The Old Bell (01666 822344) has an Edwardian restaurant with a classic Anglo-French menu. There are outside tables in summer, but on busy weekends you'll need a reservation for the dining room. A few miles east of Malmesbury, gorgeous Whatley Manor (01666 822888) also has two excellent eateries: splash out on one of chef Martin Burge's French tasting menus in The Dining Room, or have a relaxed Sunday lunch at Le Mazot, an informal brasserie.

GET A ROOM!

For more information, or to book this hotel, go to www.mrandmrssmith.com. Register your Smith membership card (see pages 4–5) to enjoy exclusive offers and privileges.

 SMITH MEMBER OFFER Rectory Cocktail in the hotel bar.

Rectory Hotel Crudwell, Malmesbury, Wiltshire SN16 9EP (01666 577194; www.therectoryhotel.com)

Cheltenham

Thirty Two

STYLE Listed Regency townhouse
SETTING Tree-lined Cheltenham square

'Stanley, a beautiful red-collared Dalmatian, matches the decor. Was the house decorated to match the dog, or vice versa?'

original fittings and stylish stand-out pieces collected from around the world. Indeed, you can buy many of the beautiful objects that populate the house; perfect for last-minute gift purchases or, for the more Puckish, a fantastic game of 'how much for that, then?' My tussle with the 400kg cranium has just taken place in the showroom on the ground floor of the house; a veritable Conran's cave of amazing stuff found, restored or designed by the pair. And, with the deity's head no longer teetering, the balance of karma seems thankfully restored. Ohmmm.

As the friendly and enthusiastic Jonathan Number One continues with our pre-check-in tour, Mrs Smith gets into an aesthetic tizzy in the main living room, discussing pieces of furniture and gleaning tips for the renovation of our flat. Bathed in sunlight from the huge sash windows, the chandeliers have been nickel-dipped and, according to Jonathan, will be 'perfectly tarnished' in about six months' time. There's a huge, eBay-purchased dining table, and de rigueur decor mags are splayed on sumptuous poufs. Sitting in the vast, super-comfortable sofa makes us wonder if we need check into our room at all. While Jonathan and Mrs Smith continue to share their mutual love of junk shops, I grab the bags and make a run for it.

Our super king-size suite is situated on the top floor, involving a trip upstairs that will keep any visiting butts Stairmaster-toned. There's a view of the Imperial Gardens (the only room to boast such a treat, we're secretly smug to discover), while a gorgeous glass writing table, huge pieces of wooden furniture and floor-to-ceiling lengths of silk serve as an advert for the Jonathans' design business. And to the bathroom: a fire-placed affair, with a bath poised and ready for soaking in whilst enjoying views through the window over the beautiful square. As we get ready to explore outside, the equally affable Other Jonathan returns with Stanley: a beautiful red-collared Dalmatian that spookily matches the decor of the house. As we leave, questions tease us: was the house decorated to match the dog, or vice versa? Is the dog for sale?

Despite the recent awful weather (the area was battered by the summer floods of 2007), we've arrived on the hottest day of the year and the whole town (or at least

The Buddha's head is huge. Approximately three feet in diameter, and intricately carved from solid marble, it was transported all the way from India to Cheltenham. In fact, it took six people to heave it onto the display plinth it now occupies. I dare not ask its price, particularly as it's wobbling almost uncontrollably on said plinth – a direct result of my child-like inability to not touch things I shouldn't. Owner Jonathan is remarkably calm. 'Yes, it can be a little unsteady,' he says as I grapple with the beast, barely managing to bring it to heel.

Thirty Two is a five-star, four-room townhouse retreat in the heart of Cheltenham, towering over the main Imperial Square gardens. It's owned and run by 'the two Jonathans', aka Jonathan Sellwood and Jonathan Parkin, interior designers formerly based in London, who have created a hotel that 'feels like visiting a friend's home'. Evidence of the pair's trade is everywhere: the house is an impeccable blend of ancient and Noughties furniture, those who haven't nipped off to Cornwall for the weekend) is taking advantage of the sunshine. We decide to join the loafing students, young families and the closest an affluent town like Cheltenham has to chavs in the Imperial Gardens to bask for a while. This Mr Smith wastes no time in going native and is soon bare-chested, face down and snoozing off his third glass of Sancerre from the Wild Duck Inn, the 16th-century Cotswolds pub in Ewen that we lunched at earlier. A faint smell of weed permeates the air, frisbees are thrown, sun is shined and sweet nothings whispered. Niceness.

'Frisbees are thrown, sun is shined and sweet nothings whispered. Niceness'

Our evening consists of a fantastic meal at Monty's Brasserie on St George's Road, which also has a vibrant basement cocktail bar, followed by drinks at quirky Hotel Kandinsky's atrium bar. We wander the near-deserted streets in a pleasant, boozy fug around midnight. The town is relatively quiet during our visit, but we hear it truly comes alive during the many festivals it hosts – especially at the Imperial Square gardens opposite the hotel.

The following day we return to the Cotswolds, visiting Charles and Camilla's 'hood near Tetbury. We even pay a visit to Shipton Mill, where all the flour for Charlie's organic Duchy Originals biscuits is produced. It's also the workplace of Mrs Smith's mum, who's particularly pleased as her dahlias have just scooped first prize in the Tetbury Flower Show. We break out some Duchy chocolate gingers to celebrate.

Like many visitors to Thirty Two, we've used the place as a stop-off point on our trans-Britain road trip to Cornwall. Next time, it may well be our final destination. After helping us with our bags as we depart, both Jonathans and Stanley stand on the step, waving and wagging goodbye. Like staying at a friend's house… if only we had friends this stylish.

Reviewed by Nick DeCosemo

NEED TO KNOW

Rooms Four, including three junior suites.

Rates £180–£310, including breakfast.

Check-out 11am.

Facilities In rooms, flatscreen TV, DVD/CD player, iPod dock, drinks facilities, free WiFi, bathrobes, heated mist-free mirrors, rain shower heads, Penhaligon's toiletries.

Children Kids over the age of eight are welcome, but there are no special provisions made for them.

Also This five-star B&B is a pet-free zone, with private parking for guests. Thirty Two's owners Jonathan and Jonathan run an interior-design company from the house, so if you fall for that deco-style Perspex lamp, you can probably buy it in their on-site showroom.

IN THE KNOW

Our favourite rooms Each is individually designed. Hidcote has silk-framed views across the calm expanse of Imperial Square gardens, and an enchanting bathroom with a fireplace. The new ground-floor suite is the largest with a separate sitting room, boasting copper bath and working fireplace.

Hotel bar Help yourself from the honesty bar in the Drawing Room until 10pm.

Hotel restaurant No restaurant. The Breakfast Room has a table for eight, but a Continental breakfast in bed can be ordered for those who can't face talking to anyone in the morning.

Top table The breakfast table is communal, so rise early for a fire-side seat.

Room service None, although if you want to impress the Mr or Mrs, wine, champagne and flowers can be pre-ordered, ready for your arrival.

Dress code Pad down to breakfast in your cashmere socks (but don't forget your dressing gown).

Local knowledge Nearby and perfect for picnics, Cleeve Hill is the highest point in the Cotswolds, with incredible views of the Black Mountains and across Cheltenham Racecourse.

LOCAL EATING AND DRINKING

Gusto, a deli on Montpellier Walk (01242 239111), shakes the best coffee beans in town and will pop goodies from the shop into a picnic hamper for you. Get your alfresco fix at the **Hot Pepper Jelly** café on Suffolk Road (01242 719999), which has a sun-dappled courtyard, or in the Imperial Square gardens, where an open-air bar dispenses liquid refreshments during summer. For a pre-supper spritzer or after-dinner drinks, **Thirteen Degrees** on St George's Road (01242 241144) is the perfect restored-Regency cocktail hang-out. The elegant **Lumière** on Clarence Parade serves modern 'global' cuisine and always looks lively (01242 222200), but if it's an immaculate, Michelin-starred French feast you're after, book a table at the incomparable **Le Champignon Sauvage** on Suffolk Road (01242 573449).

GET A ROOM!

For more information, or to book this hotel, go to www.mrandmrssmith.com. Register your Smith membership card (see pages 4–5) to enjoy exclusive offers and privileges.

 SMITH MEMBER OFFER 25 per cent off all drinks from the honesty bar. Plus, a 10 per cent discount on all gifts and accessories in the hotel's showroom.

Thirty Two 32 Imperial Square, Cheltenham, Gloucestershire GL50 1QZ (01242 771110; www.thirtytwoltd.com)

CUMBRIA

COUNTRYSIDE Mountains, lakes and meadows
COUNTRY LIFE Ramblers, writers and road trips

Cumbria's dramatic, brooding landscape has inspired creative souls for centuries: poet William Wordsworth penned many of his most famous works here, and it's where Beatrix Potter chose to settle with her beloved flock of Herdwick sheep. With 16 beautiful lakes, unspoilt shorelines and 100 lofty peaks more than 2,000 feet high, this is the perfect place to go wandering 'lonely as a cloud'. Silken-surfaced waters and windswept fells certainly provide a moody backdrop for the region's legion Arthurian legends and ancient stone circles: it's no wonder the Lake District is such a magnet for hopeless romantics. Be warned, though – Cumbria's good looks and pleasing manner can attract style-cramping crowds in high summer. Flirt with life beyond the bigger towns and tourist traps, and you'll be rewarded by Ruskin-approved Arts and Crafts charm and breathtaking scenery.

GETTING THERE

Planes Both Manchester (www.manchesterairport.co.uk) and Liverpool (www.liverpoolairport.com) airports are less than 90 minutes' drive away from the southern reaches of Cumbria, the Lake District. Glasgow (www.glasgowairport.com) and Edinburgh (www.edinburghairport.com) airports are a couple of hours' drive from Carlisle, in the north of the county.
Trains The West Coast Main Line (www.virgintrains.co.uk) from London to Glasgow stops at Oxenholme (change here for Kendal and Windermere), Penrith and Carlisle. Regular direct trains connect Manchester Airport and Windermere (via Oxenholme).
Automobiles The M6 from the Midlands to Carlisle passes up the eastern side of the county, providing easy access from all parts of the UK. You'll definitely want a car for exploring the Lakes.

LOCAL KNOWLEDGE

Taxis The only option is a good local minicab company; in Kirkby Lonsdale, try 24-7 Taxis (01524 273395). Your best bet is to ask your hotel to arrange drop-offs and pick-ups for you.
Packing tips Walking shoes and a waterproof jacket, in case you fancy a hike; wine cooler and picnic basket for gathering foraged foodstuffs to consume en route.
Recommended reads Historical novel *Haweswater* by Sarah Hall; some Wordsworth poetry (try Penguin's *Selected*

Poems); or Arthur Ransome's classic children's adventure *Swallows and Amazons*, set on Coniston Water.
Local specialities The region produces a wonderful array of gourmand goodies, from Cumberland sausages to Grasmere gingerbread. Yew Tree Farm Heritage Meats sells delicious cuts of Cumbrian Herdwick lamb and Belted Galloway beef. Visit the farm shop in Coniston or order fleece-lined recyclable hampers online (01539 441433; www.heritagemeats.co.uk). In Lyth Valley, Savin Hill Farm (01539 568410; www.savin-hill.co.uk) raises pure-bred British White cattle and Middle White pigs to produce its delicious marbled beef and hams.

Perfect picnic With so much hamper-compatible greenery about, it's not hard to find an idyllic spot for reclined alfresco dining. Pre-order a picnic for two from Lakeland Picnic (01539 568410) or pick up supplies from Booths in Kirkby Lonsdale (01524 273443) and head to the Crook O'Lune river banks near Caton; you may have to walk a bit to find a quiet stretch – the area's beauty is renowned. And... The Pinter-scripted scenes in *The French Lieutenant's Woman* were filmed in John Ruskin's house at Brantwood, and the rural adventure in *Withnail and I* was filmed around the Cumbrian towns of Penrith and Shap. 'We've gone on holiday by mistake...'

WORTH GETTING OUT OF BED FOR

Viewpoint Climb up Bowfell, a mountain in the Lakeland fells with commanding views of the Pennines to the east and the Isle of Man to the west. More experienced and armed with mint cake? Conquer England's highest peak, the rugged 978-metre Scafell Pike, at Wasdale.

Arts and culture Book-lovers, head to Wordsworth's Dove Cottage in Grasmere (www.wordsworth.org.uk), and Beatrix Potter's farmhouse, Hill Top, in Ambleside (www.nationaltrust.org.uk). Blackwell House in Bowness-on-Windermere (www.blackwell.org.uk) is a beautiful Arts and Crafts building with exhibitions and a lovely tearoom. Abbot Hall in Kendal (www.abbothall. org.uk) is an attractive gallery with skilfully curated exhibitions; for buzzier cultural events, go to the nearby Brewery Arts Centre (www.breweryarts.co.uk).

Activities On sunny days, there's no nicer way to cruise Windermere's waters than aboard the 50-foot luxury motor yacht *Mistress* (07717 207583; www. lakedistrictboatcharter.co.uk); charter her exclusively from £495. Try rock-climbing, abseiling or ghyll scrambling with guides from Climb365 (www.climb365. net), who set up shop in the Lake District for summer. Hot-air balloon trips along the Lune Valley from Wray Village are spectacular (www.virginballoonflights.co.uk).

Daytripper On Cumbria's fringe, the Western Yorkshire Dales stretch south and east, and are often far less busy than the lakes themselves. Get a soothing eyeful of soft-edged gorges in the spectacular Mallerstang dale, just south of little-visited town Kirkby Stephen. It's also the site of the ruined Pendragon Castle, supposedly founded by King Arthur's father – so let your imagination go gallivanting off into the sunset with those dashing knight/distressed damsel fantasies.

Children The little ones can have their own *Swallows and Amazons*-style adventures with sailing lessons at Coniston Boating Centre (01539 441366; www.lake-district.gov.uk). Kendal Museum (www.kendalmuseum.org.uk) has plenty of child-friendly exhibits and organises a slew of activities during school holidays.

Walks Fill your boots with a pub lunch at the Fish Hotel in the village of Buttermere (01768 770253) before tackling the hike up to Scale Force, the Lake District's highest waterfall (almost 52 metres in total).

Shopping There are treasures to be had beyond the Beatrix Potter tea towels and Kendal mint cake – keep an eye out for little antiques shops. Booths (www. booths-supermarkets.co.uk) is a small chain of delis specialising in delicious Cumbrian produce; there are outlets in Kirkby Lonsdale, Windermere and Kendal.

Something for nothing Head to Keswick and visit the Castlerigg Stone Circle, an inscrutable arrangement of 48 craggy stones with dramatic views over to Skiddaw, Blencathra and Lonscale Fell. For leafy adventure, follow a trail through Grizedale Forest Park and find a glade from where you can gaze out over Coniston Water, Windermere and Grizedale Valley (01229 860010).

Don't go home without... admiring Ruskin's View – a spot overlooking the Lune River so named because it captivated that most discerning of Victorian thinkers. It's in Kirkby Lonsdale, behind the St Mary's church graveyard (not as ghoulish as it sounds). Drink it all in, then go for a drink at the Snooty Fox Inn (01524 271308).

COMPLETELY CUMBRIAN

Created by accident when a pan of glacier-mint mixture was left unattended by a distracted Kendal confectioner, mint cake first went into production in 1869 and was an instant (sugar) hit. Vigorous outdoors types have used it to keep them on the march ever since it was supplied to Shackleton's Antarctic expedition, and a batch from Romney's of Kendal famously accompanied Sir Edmund Hillary to the summit of Everest. Get your fix at the Sweet Shop in Kirkby Lonsdale's Market Square (01524 271570; www.uksweetsshop.co.uk).

DIARY

April St George's Day parade in Kirkby Lonsdale. June The Westmorland Country Fest is one of the region's biggest foodie events, with attractions including cookery demonstrations, beer festival and terrier races (www.westmorlandshow.co.uk). August Grasmere Sports & Show, including old-school Cumberland and Westmorland Wrestling, frantic hound trails and hard-fought tug-of-war contests (http://grasmeresportsandshow.co.uk). September World Gurning Championships – we kid you not – at the Egremont Crab Fair & Sports in Egremont (www.egremontcrabfair.org.uk).

Kirkby Lonsdale

Hipping Hall

STYLE Historic fine dining
SETTING Verdant Lune Valley

'We were in the dales: picture-book church, daffodils, wagging lambs' tails. And mud. Which goes to show, you can't pack too many shoes for a weekend in the country'

This isn't something I'm proud to admit, but I am completely incapable of being grown-up about bad weather on holiday. A rainy day or an overcast sky, and my mood quickly turns blacker than the darkest thunderstorm. I have cried in Capri, thrown tantrums in Tuscany and wept in Wales. So the prospect of an early April weekend in Lancashire didn't look promising. For the sake of the long-suffering Mr Smith, Hipping Hall was going to have to be good.

Our carriage pulled out of the train station beneath a sky the colour of over-washed undies, and eventually emerged to a bright and freshly laundered Lancaster. Driving the final 30 minutes to Hipping Hall, our spirits lifted with the clouds as they melted away. A cluster of ivy-clad stone buildings set in three acres of greenery, Hipping Hall is a lovingly restored 17th-century house in a 15th-century hamlet. Nestled in the romantic-sounding Lune Valley, this hotel and restaurant is a mere stone's throw away from the majesty of Wordsworth's lakes and the wilderness of the Brontës' moors.

Pulling up outside the entrance, we were greeted by the 29-year-old proprietor, Andrew Wildsmith (his real name, not a pseudonym borrowed from a dashing Brontë hero), who swapped a PhD in organic chemistry at Cambridge for the challenge of causing a few reactions with a hotel experiment back home.

We found our room to be both simple and luxurious: no frills or florals to make Mr Smith nervous; and much to please the fussier Mrs Smith – in particular, the magnificent centrepiece of a white-canopied bed. Light pours in through windows overlooking the front garden, with its whispering fountain and well-groomed lawn, and the minimally elegant bathroom is styled in limestone (all Hipping Hall's bathrooms feature a different natural stone), with a deep, double-ended bath.

In contrast to the soothing neutrals and airy tranquillity of the hotel's nine bedrooms, the reception room, bar and lounge are strikingly opulent, with just a dash of kitsch – the inspiration of homegrown interior designer James Mackie, whose creative credentials include playing

keyboards for Madness and the Selector. The style is country house (flock wallpaper, gilt mirrors, oil paintings) meets Soho House (sofas in clashing colours and patterns, leather armchairs in pillar-box red). This is a rural retreat where a city girl can feel right at home.

There was just time for a stroll before dinner. Within moments of setting foot outside we were deep in the dales: gentle lanes, a picture-book church, hosts of daffodils and wagging lambs' tails. And mud. Oh dear – those immaculate white carpets... It just goes to show, you can't pack too many pairs of shoes for a weekend in the country.

Hipping Hall defines itself as a restaurant with rooms, and the well-informed come from all around just for supper. New Zealander chef Brent Hulena trained at leading luxury hotel Huka Lodge, and he uses local ingredients from nearby farms with imagination. Dining under the high-vaulted eaves of the 15th-century banqueting hall – the oak beams are from old ships – is an experience in

itself: if it doesn't get your weekend off to a romantic start, nothing will. Although the menu is as extravagant as the surroundings, much of the fresh produce comes from a nearby farm. Sticky pig's cheek, halibut and oxtail, Kitridding lamb... all by firelight.

And still, the highlight of my evening was yet to come, even with Mr Smith already fast asleep. What a bed – fit for a king and queen, with an extra-soft second mattress and cloudy pillows: one firm, one fluffy. I slept like the fabled princess would have if it hadn't been for that pesky pea. Sunday, the weather was filthy. But let it rain! After a late breakfast, it was straight back to my super-snug bed with the newspapers.

Later, with a little persuasion from Mr Smith, and two huge Hipping Hall golfing brollies, we braved the elements to visit the waterfalls of Ingleton – another fairy-tale place name. It was gratifying to follow up our feasting with an invigorating yomp outdoors, but we were soon drying off in front of the fire, with a pot of tea and home-made cherry cake. As a drippy (in every sense) Andie MacDowell once said to Hugh Grant, 'Is it still raining? I hadn't noticed.' By the end of our stay, I couldn't have given a damn what the weather was doing; I now know how to combine contentment with a wet weekend...

Reviewed by Lisa Allardice

'Dining under the high-vaulted eaves of the 15th-century banqueting hall – oak beams from old ships – is an experience in itself'

NEED TO KNOW

Rooms Nine: six in the main house; three in a cottage across the courtyard.

Rates £120–£250, including breakfast.

Check-out 11am, but pretty flexible; earliest check-in, 3pm.

Facilities Handmade beds, Vi-Spring mattresses, flatscreen TVs, CD players, underfloor heating in bathrooms, and toiletries by the Bath House in Sedbergh.

Children Kids are welcome, though there is no special menu in the restaurant. There is a foldaway bed, and Room 6 has a sofa bed, with an extra charge only if your child is having dinner.

Also Guests with a small and well-behaved dog can be accommodated in the duplex cottage room. There's usually a two-night minimum stay on Saturdays, but check for late availability.

IN THE KNOW

Our favourite rooms Light and spacious Room 2 has exposed beams, a limestone bathroom and views of the garden. High-ceilinged Room 4 is also airy and big, overlooking the front garden. Room 6 is the largest in the main house, with a separate snug sofa area, and its natural-stone, garden-view bathroom has a big whirlpool bath. In the cottage, split-level Room 7 has a spiral staircase leading up to the bedroom and bathroom.

Hotel bar Residents can relax at all hours in the oak-panelled bar, by the fire or looking out over the landscaped gardens.

Hotel restaurant Under high-vaulted eaves in a 15th-century banqueting hall with a minstrels' gallery, you can feast on New Zealander Brent Hulena's modern take on traditional rustic classics. Seasonal veg are plucked straight from Hipping Hall's walled garden. Last orders: 1.45pm for lunch; 9.30pm for dinner.

Top table In front of the fire in winter, or on the balcony in summer.

Room service Drinks only, from 7.45am until 11.30pm.

Dress code Loosen your collar as much as you like.

Local knowledge Visit the Ingleton waterfalls and caves (www.ingletonwaterfalls.co.uk) and drop by Wordsworth's Dove Cottage en route (www.wordsworth.org.uk). Get high on the astonishing views from the basket of a hot-air balloon as it floats above the Lune Valley with Virgin Balloon Flights (www.virginballoonflights.co.uk).

LOCAL EATING AND DRINKING

With freshly baked bread and home-made fruit scones hot from the oven, The Cariad coffee house and tearoom in Kirkby Lonsdale (01524 273271) will set you up for an afternoon of sightseeing. The Samling is a 40-minute drive away, just outside Ambleside (01539 431922). It has a spectacular setting with views over Wordsworth's beloved hills, and a fantastic menu. A little closer to Hipping Hall is the art-filled Avanti Bar & Restaurant in Kirkby Lonsdale (01524 273500), which offers the full Cumbrian experience thanks to comforting meat and fish dishes, and homely touches without the slightest hint of twee.

GET A ROOM!

For more information, or to book this hotel, go to www.mrandmrssmith.com. Register your Smith membership card (see pages 4–5) to enjoy exclusive offers and privileges.

 SMITH MEMBER OFFER A gift box of toiletries from the Bath House of Sedbergh.

DEVON

COUNTRYSIDE Pastures, parks and promenades
COUNTRY LIFE Cream tea by the sea

Devon is the stuff of childhood dreams. Sun-kissed beaches and quiet little coves hark back to a time when all you needed for a day of unbridled pleasure was a bucket and spade, acres of sand and the promise of an ice-cream before bed. Today, surf's up for a new generation of coastal devotees, keen to rediscover rural delights without abandoning urban expectations. And not just on the beach, either: Dartmoor, in all its ruggedly spartan glory, provides the county with a dramatic, windswept heart (perfect for walking, riding and cycling) that's serviced by a swathe of picturesque villages. Gastronomically, Devon punches well above its weight, with clotted-cream teas and a rich pantry of home-grown produce – all readily proffered by an ever-spreading spate of fine new restaurants keen to make the most of the fact that, on every level, Devon delivers.

GETTING THERE

Planes Your best bet in these parts is Plymouth airport: Air Southwest (www.airsouthwest.com) flies there from London Gatwick, Manchester, Leeds, Bristol and Jersey.
Trains There are regular trains from London Paddington to Exeter and Plymouth with First Great Western (www.firstgreatwestern.co.uk); journeys take just over three hours. Virgin Trains (www.virgintrains.co.uk) also connects Plymouth to London, as well as other regional hubs such as Newcastle, Leeds and Glasgow.
Automobiles Drive from the London orbital to Exeter in under four hours (traffic permitting) on the A303. The M5 connects Devon to the north via Bristol (90 minutes) and Birmingham (three hours). A car is invaluable once there, for pootling along the coast or country-lane cruising.

LOCAL KNOWLEDGE

Taxis Even at train stations, it can be hard to find a cab, so book your pick-ups ahead. Plymouth Taxis (01752 606060) is a licensed fleet of wheelchair-friendly London cabs. In Tavistock, try Jay Cars (07860 298808).
Packing tips If you've got one, a wetsuit is handy for braving the bracing English Channel waters, whether you're surfing the waves or just swimming. Otherwise, general outdoorsy gear is likely to serve you well.
Recommended reads Read Arthur Conan Doyle's spine-chiller *The Hound of the Baskervilles* then head for Dartmoor and see if you don't get a bit scared... Poet Alice Oswald's award-winning *Dart* creates a rich narrative around the Devon river. Agatha Christie's page-turning whodunnit *Evil Under the Sun* is based on Burgh Island.
Local specialities Don't come expecting to count calories: you're in clotted cream's heartland. With a cream tea on every menu, settle all jam-or-dairy-on-first arguments with the trivial knowledge that, in Devon, the white stuff goes on first (it's the other way round in Cornwall). Thanks to the mild climate, Devon's cup runneth over with vineyards; embark on your own *Sideways*-style wine-tasting trail – go to www.visitdevon.com to see suggested itineraries. The region's local seafood is also excellent.
Perfect picnic With the expanse of moorland and two coastlines of beaches to choose from, finding a quiet spot is never a problem. Acquire supplies from award-winning NH Crebers Delicatessen, a Tavistock purveyor of local cheeses and freshly ground coffee (01822 612266).

WORTH GETTING OUT OF BED FOR

Viewpoint At 621 metres, High Willhays on Dartmoor is the highest point in southern England, and unsurprisingly offers panoramic views across remote open country. Avoid the area if you see any raised red flags, though: the Army flies them when when it does training here.

Arts and culture Saltram House in Plympton (01752 333500) is a grand Georgian home with exquisite gardens and astonishing interiors, including paintings by Reynolds. The National Trust property may look familiar: it was used to represent the Dashwoods' pad in the film of *Sense and Sensibility*. Buckland Abbey in Yelverton (01822 853607), once the home of serial roamer Sir Francis Drake, is all Tudor splendour and landmark gardens. If you like your culture prehistoric, head to Dartmoor, which has more Bronze Age standing stones, known as menhirs, than anywhere else in the country. The Beardown Man near Devil's Tor is an especially ominous example.

Activities Surf's up. Croyde on the north coast has worth-it waves, and lessons, board hire and encouragement are on hand from the Barefoot Surf School (www.barefootsurf. com). Dry-land lovers can hire a bike from Tavistock Cycles (01822 617630) and explore the moors on two wheels. Or, take to the Tarka Trail (www.devon.gov.uk/ tarkatrail), 30 miles of largely traffic-free cycling along former railway routes – try Otter Cycle Hire in Braunton (01271 813339). Alternatively, indulge your inner *Swallows and Amazons* and mess about in boats on the Tamar River: from Saltash, TamarSail will take you out on their traditional gaff-rigged craft (www.tamarsail.co.uk).

Daytripper The Cornish fishing village of Padstow is about an hour's drive along the A30. It's often referred to as 'Padstein', thanks to the culinary influences of a certain Rick Stein, whose eatery empire runs the gamut from fine dining to delis. Grab grilled mackerel and chips from Stein's Fish & Chips on South Quay – you definitely won't want to share them with the seagulls (www.rickstein. com). Green-keen tourists should check out the Eden Project, which offers first-hand, environmentally friendly access to the world's flora. The Warm Temperate Biome is particularly comforting when the weather's bad (www.edenproject.com).

Children Devon is all about ice-creams, buckets and spades, and sand in your shoes. The best coastal destinations for children are the beaches of South Hams – Bigbury and Blackpool Sands are clean and safe. If it rains, Pennywell Farm and Wildlife Centre (www.pennywellfarm.co.uk) has everything from piglets to ponies to keep boredom at bay; or, youngsters can lose themselves in the spider's-web-like willow maze.

Walks Dartmoor's on your doorstep and has 368 square miles of open wilderness. On a sunny day, the views are incomparable, but in winter, the mist can wrap around you in no time, so take warm waterproofs and a phone. Map-reading skills not so hot? Book a guide from the National Park Authority (www.dartmoor-npa.gov.uk).

Shopping Tavistock's Farmers' Market, normally on the second and fourth Saturdays of each month, is a great place to go browsing and grazing (www.tavistockfarmers market.com). Otherwise, visit a local farm shop: Beeches Farm (01822 833661) is known for its rare-breed pork, sold from the farm gate. Cheesephiles can sample then select their chunk of Little Stinky or Devon Sage at Country Cheeses in Tavistock (01822 615035). Marystow Farm Enterprises (01822 860420) in Lifton only makes between 12 and 20 jars of handmade jams and condiments at a time on its Aga; be naughty and pass them off as your own.

Something for nothing The 27-metre White Lady waterfall at Lydford Gorge near Okehampton is a spectacular sight, and a rewarding one for anyone who walks along the arduous but lushly beautiful ravine. Look out for kingfishers.

Don't go home without... imbibing some local cider. Countryman Ciders, located in a 15th-century stable block in Tavistock (01822 870226), has an amazing array of apple-based ales to try before you buy.

DETERMINEDLY DEVON

Dartmoor is the home of letterboxing. No, it doesn't involve carparks: this bizarre 'sport' mixes orienteering with grown-up treasure hunt, and is based on messages left in 'letterboxes' dotted around the moors. Each one contains a visitors' book, an inked stamp to prove you've found it, and clues to the whereabouts of the next one. Some granite 'letterboxes' date from the 1830s; modern ones are likely to be old Army ammunition tins (www.dartmoorletterboxing.org).

DIARY

March Exeter Festival of South West England Food & Drink hails local produce (www.visit southwest.co.uk). **May/June** English Wine Week is celebrated all over, but Devon's many vineyards make it one of the best places for tasting events and tours (www.englishwineweek. co.uk). **June** North Devon Festival, centred in Barnstaple, hosts live music, food, theatre and literature events (www.northdevonfestival.org). **June** Goldcoast Oceanfest worships sun, sea and surfing in Croyde Bay (www.goldcoastoceanfest.co.uk). **July** The Port Eliot Lit Fest, held in a stately home near Saltash, draws big names from the art, music and cabaret worlds (www.porteliotfestival.com). **October** Tavistock's annual Goose Fair has attracted traders since the 12th century, but the two-day event is no longer restricted to poultry shifters: today, stallholders from all over the country descend to sell and to entertain (www.tavistock.gov.uk).

Milton Abbot

Hotel Endsleigh

STYLE Fairy-tale fishing lodge
SETTING Unspoilt Devonshire woodland

'The grade I-listed fishing lodge is insanely pretty and the setting magical: it's easy to see why in 1812 the Bedfords decided this was the loveliest spot in the county'

one further thing in common: they look extremely happy to be where they are. And so they should, for Hotel Endsleigh is a class act. The house, a grade I-listed fishing lodge, is insanely pretty, and the setting magical: it's easy to see why the Bedford family, who at the time owned a third of Devon, decided in 1812 that this was the loveliest spot in the county on which to build their house.

From the lawned terrace, the view sweeps down to the rapid waters of the River Tamar, which divides Devon from Cornwall, and up densely wooded banks on the other side. Arriving on a snowy night, we hurried from our car in search of hot baths and long drinks. Our room, Number Seven, was one of the less grand; nonetheless, it combined the assets of a chic private house (interesting art, bedside reading) with those of a good hotel (huge bed, plasma TV), and boasted walls of a delicious duck-egg blue.

Hunger and curiosity soon coaxed us downstairs for drinks, snacks and, of course, people-watching. The ground floor is a jigsaw of cosy, characterful spaces: a drawing room with a huge log fire; a pretty sitting room with hand-painted wallpaper; a well-stocked library boasting everything from Allen Carr's *Easy Way to Stop Smoking* to the Koran, and from *The Jewel in the Crown* to *The Shadow of the Wind*; even a corridor stocked with Hunter wellies in every size, for ill-prepared townie guests.

Dinner in the wood-panelled dining room ranged from very good (roast monkfish and a fruit pancake dessert) to excellent (sea bream in watercress soup, a main of seared beef). The only low point came the next morning. Having parked our two-year-old with Grandma, our wish-list for the perfect hotel weekend began with: a lie-in. Followed by: being able to go for a walk without the promise of a playground and; browsing the papers in a country pub instead of reading *Thomas the Tank Engine* stories out loud. (A couple of elements weren't suitable for publication.) And one more wish: breakfast in bed.

So, imagine our disappointment on Saturday morning when, looking for the room-service menu, we found instead a note informing us that the Endsleigh 'discourages' in-room breakfasting, 'because our layout is not ideal.'

Y ou don't know what people-watching is until you've taken pre-dinner drinks in the bar of a smart weekenders' hotel. Forget catwalk shows, forget singles' nights – nowhere do guests check each other out with quite the same fervour witnessed over gin and tonics around 8pm every Friday at boutique boltholes all over the country. There's a good reason for this. Your choice of venue for an indulgent weekend reveals a great deal about you: not only your budget, but your taste; not just your interests, but your aspirations. In theory, these are your people.

Guests at the Hotel Endsleigh are, while style-conscious, more Boden than Balenciaga, as you'd expect of a clientele weekending in this remote, beautiful valley between Dartmoor and Bodmin Moor. They are moneyed, but of the old school that prefers roll-top baths to Jacuzzis. (I distinctly heard the gentleman savouring a brandy in the library describe it as 'scrumptious'.) And they have

In the light of this schoolmarmish diktat, we were a bit worried that Alex, the hotel's impressive but rather formidable owner, was about to burst in, throw open the shutters and chide us for wasting a glorious day, so we dressed and hurried down for breakfast. (Good coffee, creamy scrambled eggs and crunchy toast with delicious marmalade: perfect.)

But any grumpiness couldn't last. From the moment we pulled on our wellies and stepped outside, resistance was futile: we were in love with Hotel Endsleigh. By the time we had explored the garden and grounds – a satisfying two-hour walk – we were decided that it was one of the most beautiful places we had ever seen. A freak snowfall had transformed this very English scene into Narnia. A ping-pong table looked fabulously eccentric under five inches of snow; croquet hoops were half buried, while the forest of evergreens on the far side of the river bowed under their frosty burdens.

'From the moment we stepped outside, resistance was futile: we were in love with Hotel Endsleigh'

We made our way down to the tumbling, icy waters of the Tamar and back, discovering waterfalls and a picturesque shell grotto along the way. As we climbed back to the hotel, Alex's pet Vietnamese pot-bellied pig, with black spots on a pink coat, trotted through the snow to greet us. (Though, sadly, we hear he's no longer around.) We have stumbled into another world, we marvelled, four and a half hours from London.

Now a scene to truly tempt you to Endsleigh is the one that met us in the library: a cream tea laid out for guests, complete with fruit scones, Devon cream and home-made jam, and cake stands piled high with temptatations. All around, happy guests sat contentedly in armchairs, working their way through the weekend papers with pots of Earl Grey at their elbows.

The sound of our boots crunching on virgin snow as we stepped out to explore the garden, the fragrant crackle of log fires, and the glow of candlelight on a dark afternoon are all wintry delights. But then, summer must be magical too: the sloping terrace is perfect for an early evening Pimm's; the river full of salmon (the hotel has a resident 'ghillie', their own fishing expert, and expeditions are encouraged); the long croquet lawn is marvellously Gatsby-esque. With word of a swimming pool on the way, we leave with the promise that we will be back long before the next snowfall.

Reviewed by Jess Cartner-Morley

NEED TO KNOW

Rooms 16, including two suites and a gatekeeper's lodge.

Rates £180–£360, including full English breakfast. Two-night minimum stay at weekends.

Check-out 11am. Check-in, 2pm, but if you arrive earlier the porter can take care of your luggage while you explore.

Facilities The lodge is set in 108 acres of soul-enriching woodland and gardens, including a stretch of the Tamar river and a croquet lawn. Massages can be booked with 24 hours' notice. Library, free WiFi, badminton, table tennis, games. Rooms have flatscreen TVs, DVD players, and CD players on request.

Children Many rooms at this family-friendly hotel have space for an extra child's bed (£30) or cot (free). Three of the suites have sofa-beds, suitable for teenagers or extra adults (£30). Babysitting and listening can be arranged. Very young children aren't allowed in the restaurant after 7pm.

Also Picnics, horse riding, archery, clay-pigeon shooting, falconry, fishing, private guides, Pilates/yoga instruction and bicycle hire can all be arranged (some activities require advance notice). The hotel closes for two weeks every January.

IN THE KNOW

Our favourite rooms Room 8 has a marvellous garden view, as does Room 5, which also overlooks the river. You can see the river and the garden from the bathroom of Room 3. Suite 1 on the ground floor has direct access to the gardens through French doors. The Gatekeeper's Lodge has private, enclosed gardens, and a fridge for keeping that champagne ice-cold.

Hotel bar There is a 24-hour honesty bar, which includes a great selection of wines.

Hotel restaurant There are two dining rooms serving Modern European cuisine, using organic and locally sourced ingredients. The menu changes regularly to reflect the seasons. Last orders: lunch, 2.30pm; afternoon tea, 5.30pm; dinner, 10pm.

Top table In the larger dining room, ask for a table overlooking the croquet lawn. For an intimate dinner, the Quiet Room seats up to four and looks onto the pretty parterre. Outside, there's a nice sheltered nook on the Long Border Terrace.

Room service Drinks and tea available 24 hours a day. Light snacks (fruit platters, smoked salmon) available, 7am–11pm.

Dress code Groomed, but relaxed.

Local knowledge Hotel Endsleigh's spectacular location on Dartmoor's western edge makes enjoying the great outdoors as easy as falling off a picturesque, ivy-clad log. A particularly peaceful way to get an eyeful of all that outstanding natural beauty is from the water: Canoe Tamar (0845 430 1208) organises outings upriver from Morwellham Quay to Weir Head – you've a good chance of spotting kingfishers, otters, falcons and even the occasional seal.

LOCAL EATING AND DRINKING

An hour's walk along the Tamar gets you to Horsebridge, where you can rest your legs and wet your whistles at The Royal Inn (01822 870214). There's a wine bar and brasserie at Browns Hotel (01822 618686), where Modern British dishes are given a Gallic twist. At the Dartmoor Inn in Lydford (01822 820221), a series of small, airy and very chic dining rooms provide the setting for food cooked with love and imagination. The small bar does its own version of pub classics with a twist. Mix a passionate chef with local produce, an organic kitchen garden and breathtaking valley views, and you've got The Horn of Plenty in Gulworthy (01822 832528).

GET A ROOM!

For more information, or to book this hotel, go to www.mrandmrssmith.com. Register your Smith membership card (see pages 4–5) to enjoy exclusive offers and privileges.

 SMITH MEMBER OFFER Afternoon tea for two, with freshly cut sandwiches, various cakes, scones served with clotted cream and jam, and a pot of tea.

Hotel Endsleigh Milton Abbot, Tavistock, Devon PL19 0PQ (01822 870000; www.hotelendsleigh.com)

Chillington

Whitehouse

STYLE Updated Georgian abode
SETTING Charming Chillington village

'The abundance of sofas and roaring fires makes every room a perfect place for kicking back with a book or the Sunday papers after a coastal stroll'

corporate hotel: the people that work here are seldom enough seen and sufficiently sweet to make it impossible to distinguish between proprietor and employee. The hotel's owners are in fact three friends, clearly passionate about their property, each playing a hands-on role in hotel operations, and every one of them happy to address guests' requirements personally.

There are just six rooms, so I speak only for the one we stayed in, the Attic. I assume the priorities are the same – ample space, comfortable beds laden with more pillows than a princess-and-the-pea-themed photoshoot, a shower head comparable to the steering wheel of an articulated truck, and precisely the colour scheme you'd predict from the hotel's name. Make no mistake: hanging wicker chairs and rough-hewn wooden beds aside, this isn't an escape aimed at earnest hippies who prefer guitar-strumming around an open fire to revelling in contemporary comforts; our room extras included a kettle, Nespresso machine, flatscreen TV with all the Sky and DVD trimmings, a DAB radio and a well-stocked minibar. So now do you see why we just can't get excited about a tent in a wet field when it comes to our weekends away?

Perhaps a guest better versed in design might point out the most exciting style features to shout about. (Mrs Smith, for one, enthuses about its eye-pleasing modern quirks, including the old-meets-new medley of chunky furniture.) What grabbed me was the abundance of sofas and roaring fires, which make every room a perfect place for kicking back with a book or the Sunday papers after a coastal stroll. However, since my life – professional and personal – revolves around food, the headline act is always what they stick on my plate. And Whitehouse is at its best when it adheres to my most beloved cooking philosophy: take first-class ingredients, and do as little as possible to mess them up. From the just-baked scones, loaded with clotted cream and local jam, that were presented to us on arrival, through to the delicately salty Salcombe smokie (delicious mackerel, to the uninitiated) that gave breakfast a kick, via the twitchingly fresh mussels and lobster delivered to the restaurant an hour and a half before supper – the mostly local ingredients were always excellent.

It's fair to say that, reputation-wise, Devon doesn't have quite the limelight-hogging foodie allure of its neighbours,

Our visit to South Devon is due in part to our latest obsession: eating our way around Blighty – at least, as often as our busy lives and burgeoning sense of thrift allows. My beloved Mrs Smith wasn't always so prosaically monikered; her maiden name betrays Spanish origins. Yet 10 years in the UK have made her fall in love with this land. The only thing hampering the regularity of these special foodie trips is our insistence on crisp white cotton sheets and access to decent Chablis and brandy. England's way to our heart is through our stomachs, and I'm afraid camping just won't cut it. As for our favoured type of staff – we prefer those who tread that fine line between tending to your every need and leaving you alone in peace and quiet.

Just a short meander from the Devon shoreline, hidden away in the little village of Chillington, Whitehouse is the ideal getaway for style-seasoned city types hankering for a rustic rest stop. It is the opposite of a big, soulless

Dorset and Cornwall, but the county is doing its best to redress the balance, and certainly makes a stab at answering my Iberian Mrs Smith's most-posed culinary question: 'Why is it so hard to get decent fish on these shores?' Devon's response is threefold: a) you can if you try (you just have to know where to look: try the Seahorse in nearby Dartmouth); b) we don't cook fish that well (although the aforementioned seafood restaurant was the best I've been to in England); and c) because quality here is unappreciated: the majority of exceptional fish caught off Devon's coast is exported to Italy and (ironically) Spain, where consumers are happy to pay more for excellence.

As you can imagine, this fish-loving pair spent much of the weekend seeking out the perfect crustacea. So if crab, scallop or lobster float your boat, I'd urge you to do the same. But if being piscivorous isn't your thing, you could maybe plump for some pampering instead: the Whitehouse has an arrangement with the Elemis-enhanced Dart Marina Spa, 20 minutes or so away, where you can get all the treatments that five-star grooming might demand. Alternatively, stay put and play croquet on the lawn of the hotel (darling), or catch a film in the screening room. If wanderlust gets the better of you, hours spent driving or rambling through the winding country lanes nearby will be well spent.

'Whitehouse is the ideal getaway for style-seasoned city types hankering for a rustic rest stop'

Whitehouse is so much more than a common-or-garden fancy hotel; it's welcoming to the point that a stay here feels like spending the weekend with stylish, hospitable (and significantly better off) friends. Its appearance is the result of the owners' good taste rather than the work of an interior designer, and it's more a place to feel comfortable in than marvel at. These Georgian buildings have been a doctor's surgery, a residence for GIs, and a private home in their time, but today they've finally found their true calling as one of Devon's most welcoming and intimate boutique hotels. Sure there was the occasional slip-up, but to moan about a forgotten dish, say, would be missing the point.

We were looking for something unmistakably English. And we were lucky enough to find a homely, eccentric hideaway in the middle of a splendid county that is showcasing its food and drink heritage better than ever. And don't let its American-presidential-abode name distract: this hotel makes you feel truly patriotic. Rule Britannia, indeed.

Reviewed by Will Beckett

NEED TO KNOW

Rooms **Six.**

Rates £180–£250, including full English or Continental breakfast, afternoon tea. You can rent the whole house (sleeping 12) for two nights from £2,600; additional nights cost £1,300 each.

Check-out Midday, although this may be flexible (subject to availability). Check-in, 2pm.

Facilities Croquet lawn, gardens, chest of DVDs and CDs, screening room, free WiFi throughout. In rooms: plasma TVs, CD/DVD player with iPod connection, Nespresso machine. In-room beauty treatments can be arranged.

Children Kids are welcome (but not in the restaurant after 6pm); cots (£10) and extra beds (£25, with breakfast) can be added to your room. Babysitting with a local nanny costs £15 an hour.

Also A two-night minimum stay applies at weekends. Well-behaved dogs are welcome: beds, bowls and towels are provided for £10 a night – just give notice (so they can let the resident lurchers and Siamese cats know they'll have company).

IN THE KNOW

Our favourite rooms Room Five seduced us the most, with its generous size, double-aspect views of the gardens, courtyard and surrounding countryside, retro lamps and sleek metallic wallpaper. Room Four may be smaller, but the hand-crafted wooden four-poster and the free-standing French claw-foot bath had our eyes wide. The Attic room can alternate between a double and a twin – and the sofa bed means it can sleep four if you have kids or friends in tow.

Hotel bar The Whitehouse bar has a cosy living room, with shelves stuffed with travel books, a large chocolate-brown sofa and a fireside snug. It's un-Devonishly buzzy at weekends, with a different house cocktail mixed up every day.

Hotel restaurant The chef clearly has a fondness for sharing, producing a terrific array of grazing-perfect goodies served on hefty wooden boards – the star turns are cured meats, local cheeses and artisan breads. There's a daily changing menu of fresh seafood and local meat, served in the airy barn-style dining area.

Top table Secure a spot by the window overlooking the gardens. Better still, sit outside on the terrace (weather permitting).

Room service As well as the restaurant menu (available during kitchen opening hours), a selection of comfort foods such as pasta, sandwiches or Marmite on toast can be brought to your room between 11am and 11pm.

Dress code Casual but groomed; Alice Temperley with your favourite denim?

Local knowledge You can pick up a delicious deli-style picnic at Whitehouse and head off to the beach: it's a one-mile walk. Hotel staff will also be happy to arrange spa treatments, either in your room or at the Dart Marina Spa (01803 837182).

LOCAL EATING AND DRINKING

Being a wee 'pub and a post office' type of village, Chillington is hardly a haven for gastronomes, but there's plenty to tempt in nearby Dartmouth. Famed fishmonger and restaurateur Mitch Tonks is behind The Seahorse (01803 835147), a relaxed Mediterranean seafood outfit on the riverbank. The New Angel (01803 839425) serves Michelin-starred Modern Brit fare; Rumour (01803 864682) is a young and buzzy little wine bar in Totnes, which does a palatable line in pizza. In the pretty village of South Pool, The Millbrook Inn (01548 531581) continues the tradition of cider-soused West Country pubs, but throws a militantly local menu into the mix. Over in East Prawle, The Pig's Nose (01548 511209) is a great place to catch local live bands. And sister establishments to the Whitehouse worth a visit are South Milton Beach Café (01548 560844) near Salcombe and Stokely Barton Farm Shop (01548 581010), a food store, café, homeware and garden centre, a 10-minute walk away through the countryside.

GET A ROOM!

For more information, or to book this hotel, go to www.mrandmrssmith.com. Register your Smith membership card (see pages 4–5) to enjoy exclusive offers and privileges.

 SMITH MEMBER OFFER One product from Whitehouse's handmade organic toiletries range.

Whitehouse Chillington, Devon TQ7 2JX (01548 580505; www.whitehousedevon.com)

NIGHT

MORNING

DORSET

COUNTRYSIDE Hardy's hills, coastal thrills
COUNTRY LIFE From beach to pub to cricket field

Dorset is a tale of two landscapes: the chalky downlands of Cranborne Chase and the Purbeck Hills, with their pretty villages and grand houses; and the wild, adventure-friendly Jurassic Coast, rebranded but untamed. Uniting the two are this sunny county's sunny disposition and approachable nature, not to mention a market renaissance that has Dorset's bakeries, kitchens and restaurants catching up with its breweries and orchards. A single weekend down here can take you from ocean-view hike to Bridport brasserie; from Iron Age hill fort to sailing lessons in Poole Harbour (the second largest in the world). Neither London-on-sea trendy, nor too remote for a quick getaway, Dorset's resorts and countryside are favourites for natural beauty, fair weather and good old-fashioned fun.

GETTING THERE

Planes Bournemouth International Airport (www.bournemouthairport.com) has links with many European cities particularly in Spain and Italy. There is a shuttle bus that connects the airport to Bournemouth railway station (www.yellowbuses.co.uk).

Trains From London, the South Western Main Line runs down to Bournemouth, Poole, Dorchester and Weymouth; or there's the West of England Main Line, which passes through Sherborne. Go to www.national rail.co.uk to plan your journey.

Automobiles Not a single motorway carves through Dorset; from London, take the M3 to Andover or Winchester, then it's A roads all the way.

LOCAL KNOWLEDGE

Taxis The number for the main taxi rank outside Bournemouth railway station is 01202 556166. In Bridport, we recommend Beeline Taxis (01308 425555); in Dorchester, Pete's Cabs (01305 251122).

Packing tips Bring a DVD of *The French Lieutenant's Woman* to watch in bed: the adaptation of John Fowles' novel was shot on location on the Cobb at Lyme Regis. Do pack beach paraphernalia: swimwear in summer; bucket and spade in spring/autumn; kite in winter.

Recommended reads The aforementioned John Fowles novel; or one of the Thomas Hardy triumvirate – *The Mayor of Casterbridge*, *Tess of the D'Urbervilles* and *Jude*

the Obscure (for 'Casterbridge', read Dorchester; 'Shaston' stands for Shaftesbury).

Local specialities Look out for Moores Dorset Knob biscuits, Dorset apple cake, Abbotsbury rock oysters from the Fleet, Dorset Blue Vinny cheese, Wolfeton cider, and local ales from Hall & Woodhouse (www.hall-woodhouse.co.uk). Lettuce soup was traditionally made to make the most of the county's summer-harvest glut, but Dorset producers are proudest of their lamb and seafood.

Perfect picnic Head for the coast. Our favourite beaches are around the Isle of Purbeck: Kimmeridge Bay has a sheltered bay where you can dive in or just laze alongside

your alfresco fare, and the popular pebbly crescent of Lulworth Cove has rock pools to play among.

And... Standing proud on a hillside halfway between Dorchester and Sherborne, the Cerne Abbas Giant, he of the mighty prehistoric truncheon (ahem), is fenced off and just not as satisfying to see from the next-door field as he looks on postcards.

WORTH GETTING OUT OF BED FOR

Viewpoint Golden Cap, at 191 metres, is the highest point along the whole of the south coast. A stiff hike will be rewarded with stupendous views; however, a drive up to Langdon Hill carpark, via the village of Morecombelake on the A35 between Lyme and Bridport, will be rewarded similarly – once you've walked through the woods a bit.

Arts and culture Dorchester is the centre of the Thomas Hardy industry – it's the county town of South Wessex (his name for Dorset, inspired by the name of an Anglo-Saxon kingdom) – with Hardy's Cottage at Bockhampton (www.nationaltrust.org.uk), and Max Gate, the Victorian villa where he wrote *Tess of the D'Urbervilles* and *Jude the Obscure*. Bridport is becoming a cultural hub to reckon with, thanks to the new Electric Palace, an art-house cinema and brasserie backed by Richard Eyre, Mike Leigh and local Oscar-winner Julian Fellowes (www.electricpalace.org.uk). In classical music, the Bournemouth Symphony Orchestra (www.bsolive.com) is an international name, and its Summer Fireworks Proms are terrific.

Activities There's good, clean fun such as beach volleyball and water sports aplenty to be had at smart seaside resort Sandbanks. From the Cobb at Lyme Regis, you can embark on family-friendly mackerel-fishing trips with Harry May, a local skipper (07974 753287). Alternatively, speed along the heritage coastline in, on or behind a boat: Lyme Bay RIB Charter offers waterskiing, wakeboarding, day trips, sunset cruises and water taxis (www.lymebayribcharter.co.uk).

Daytripper Not quite an island, the Isle of Purbeck is a whole holiday in itself, with charmingly timewarpy Swanage, from whence a heritage railway runs to dramatic Corfe Castle; the famous sea arch at Durdle Door; and pretty Lulworth Cove, crowded in high summer but lovely to have to yourself on a wintry day.

Children The mass feeding of 600 swans at Abbotsbury Swannery near Weymouth, twice a day (at noon and 4pm), is a diverting spectacle. At the right time of year there'll be fluffy, daft-looking cygnets to charm even the hardest-hearted of your offspring. There is a children's farm here, too, where you can cuddle, ride and feed the resident furry fellows (www.abbotsbury-tourism.co.uk). Studland Bay's soft sandy beach at Purbeck is good for swimming and is family-friendly – there's a National Trust café-cum-shop for all those forgotten beach essentials.

Walks The clifftops are exhilarating (www.southwestcoastpath.com); Maiden Castle, a whopping hill fort just south of Dorchester, is fascinating to discover on foot; and for peace – solitude even – Chesil Beach is a long, long shingle spit running from Portland Bill to Abbotsbury.

Shopping Away from the high-street offerings of Weymouth, Bournemouth and Poole, Bridport lives up to its reputation as a market town, with weekly street markets on Wednesdays and Saturdays (seek out the antiques and bric-a-brac stalls on lower South Street), an excellent farmers' market in the Arts Centre on the second Saturday of every month, and a monthly antiques and second-hand book fair.

Something for nothing They call it the Jurassic Coast for a good reason: if you don't go home with your very own fossil find, you weren't looking hard enough! The sheltered stretch of Studland Bay known as Shell Bay is a good place for those who prefer to look for – you guessed it – shells.

Don't go home without... eating something from the sea at the Crab House Café in Wyke Regis (01305 788867), a no-frills former oyster depot that's highly rated by professional foodies.

DISTINCTLY DORSET

National Trust-owned Brownsea Island, the biggest of eight islands in Poole's enormous natural harbour, is a *Famous Five* setting come to life, with no cars, no towns and no dogs allowed; instead, there are red squirrels, peacocks, pinewoods and heathland. There are great views of Studland and the Isle of Purbeck, and it's no effort to get out and start walking, birdwatching (terns, herons, nightjars) or deer-spotting (www.nationaltrust.co.uk/brownsea).

DIARY

May Sherborne Abbey Festival is a week-long series of quality contemporary and classical concerts in beautiful surroundings (www.sherborneabbey.org). June Wimborne Folk Festival brings bearded trad musicians and the women who love them to the streets of this civilised Dorset community (www.wimbornefolkfestival.co.uk). Bridport Food Festival is a celebration of the locally sourced and the organically raised (www.bridportfoodfestival.org.uk).
July Larmer Tree Festival, with pop, folk and world music, fancy dress, food, massage and silly goings-on (www.larmertreefestival.co.uk). August The Great Dorset Steam Fair (www.steam-fair.co.uk) is a huge event combining – bewilderingly – heavy horses, traction engines, Punch & Judy stalls, terrifying funfair rides and pop acts. In Bournemouth, there are fireworks on the pier on Friday nights throughout August; and there's classical entertainment in the form of the Bournemouth Symphony Orchestra Classical Proms in Meyrick Park (www.bsolive.com).

Bridport

The Bull Hotel

STYLE Fresh prints, belle air
SETTING Busy little Bridport

'Beautiful roll-top baths – in our case set
on a wooden platform in the bedroom –
hit just the right note of louche decadence
for a romantic weekend away'

'When I am president of the world,' said Mr Smith, gazing about him as we stood before the open fire waiting to check into the Bull Hotel, 'all hotels will look like this.' The Bull was bought by Richard and Nikki Cooper in 2006 ('It was all a bit Fawlty Towers before then,' confides one local shopkeeper) and they've worked swiftly and successfully to restore a beloved (and grade II-listed) building to its former Georgian glory. Downstairs, the lobby, bar and gastropub restaurant are replete with stripped floorboards, wood-burning stoves, and wood panelling adorned with the duck egg/sage hues so typical of Farrow & Ball. Modern furniture, with a hint of the 1970s, provides the requisite contemporary injection.

As soon as we get to inspect the bedrooms, we see that, in here, Nikki and Richard have given themselves a freer, more extravagant hand. Cole & Son and Manuel Canovas papers feature on accent walls, setting off the shiny Philip Hunt furniture, Frette bedlinen and silk-canopied four-poster beds. And there are vintage mirrors, chests and wardrobes from Parisian fleamarkets and the antiques shops with which Bridport and its outskirts are liberally sprinkled. Beautiful roll-top baths – in our case set on a wooden platform in the bedroom – hit just the right note of louche decadence for a romantic weekend away. The bathroom itself had a huge shower, and was stocked with Neal's Yard toiletries. Other bedroom goodies include a flatscreen TV and Tivoli radio. (Mr Smith and I can't quite decide whether staying in a hotel with better shampoo and electronics than you have at home makes you feel impossibly decadent or impossibly inadequate, but we conclude it's a good conundrum to mull over while we test them all out.)

In the morning, it's shaping up to be a beautiful day. The Bull's windows are pushed up and the French doors opened, leading those who fancy breakfasting alfresco onto the suntrap of a courtyard. We linger for so long over delicious bacon, eggs and all the trimmings that we decide just to pop round the corner to the excellently named Bucky Doo Square before lunch. There, after a cup of tea in the slightly scruffy Beach & Barnicott, with its eclectic mix of clients – from cheerful Aussie hikers to a grumpy old man who may have grown out of the Georgian panelling itself – we find Bridport Old Books. This wonderful second-hand book shop

comes complete with an owner whom we witnessed gamely trying to explain Shakespearian sonnets to a teenager. Hearts warmed, we sauntered back to the Bull for lunch.

We're aware that Bridport is rapidly becoming the foodie's destination of choice: Hugh Fearnley-Whittingsall's nearby River Cottage has helped to spotlight the region's plentiful farm-and-sea-fresh produce. What we didn't realise was that the Bull employs chef Marc Montgomery. I have never been so pleased to arrive anywhere this hungry. Dinner is divine: little throaty moans of pleasure emanate from Mr Smith as he polishes off mash, gravy and sausages with more actual-factual meat in them than in most supermarkets' entire meat and poultry aisles. He assures me that similar noises could be heard from my side of the table as I tucked into beef medallions that barely needed chewing and delectably crispy potato rösti that, after a lifetime of oven-parched offerings in lesser gastropubs, were a breath of oxygen-rich fresh air. Ditto the next day's home-cured gravadlax lunch, and dinner of locally dived scallops and iced strawberry soufflé.

We justify our gargantuan appetites with a slow-paced afternoon utilising one of the Bull's more personal touches, which is that they will drop you off and pick you up at a number of the local walks in return for taking their pet spaniel, Lulu, with you. Mr Smith not only loves dogs but also windswept seaside walks. So, we spend some happy hours striding across spectacular parts of the Jurassic coast.

For our follow-up hike, after surrendering Lulu to a better Bull couple (one with energetic, stick-and-Frisbee-throwing children), we hit West Bay's pebble beach, which is bracketed by sandstone cliffs on one side and old-fashioned pubs and fish 'n' chips kiosks on the other. Walking back, we pass an elderly lady in her garden, who overhears me comment to Mr Smith on the gorgeous hot-pink flowers by the wall. 'They're wild gladioli, dear!' she trumpets gaily. 'You can't buy them in the garden centres.' She trowels up a cluster of corms and thrusts them into my hands. 'They'll spread!' she reassures. 'And that,' says Mr Smith after we've thanked her and resumed our walk, 'is why we have to move to the countryside. Londoners rarely bother giving people in the street a smile. Here, they give you flowers.'

On our final day, Lyme Regis is on our agenda. It's altogether lovely and, although I don't accrue any additions to my garden, it deserves a special mention for having been a favoured summer haunt of Jane Austen back in the day – and yet not sporting even a single 'Jamsfield Park' tea shop or gift shop devoted to selling Elizabeth Bennet tea towels and Colin Firth swimming trunks.

There's a slight chill in the air when we get back to the hotel, and the Bull has drawn itself close round its flickering fires. We curl up on the sofa in the bar, listening to the murmurs of contented diners from across the passageway, and I suddenly realise that although Bridport is in essence a seaside town, the Bull will be just as good as a cosy winter retreat. The thought that I won't have to wait until next summer to return draws the sting out of our departure. The Bull Hotel is so charming, friendly, thoughtful and relaxed – it's not just the food that makes you sigh with pleasure – we very much hate to leave. But we must. As Mr Smith reminds me, I do, after all, have gladioli to plant.

Reviewed by Lucy Mangan

NEED TO KNOW

Rooms 19, including one suite and four junior suites.

Rates £85–£235, including breakfast.

Check-out 11am, but flexible by prior arrangement; earliest check-in, 3pm.

Facilities Courtyard, games room, DVD library. Space for bicycles to be parked. In rooms, deluxe bed, flatscreen TV, DVD player, Tivoli radio in some rooms, black-out blinds, free WiFi, robes, slippers, Neal's Yard toiletries.

Children More than welcome: there are three Family Rooms with bunk beds and cots, extra beds and toy boxes can all be provided (free for under-twos; £25 a night for three-year-olds and up). Babysitting, £10 an hour.

Also The Bull Hotel has a bright and beautiful Victorian ballroom with a minstrels' gallery that can be used for wedding parties of up to 110 people. They'll also drop you off for walks if you need a lift.

IN THE KNOW

Our favourite rooms The Red Four-Poster Room (104) is the largest and will kindle romance with its vividly hued walls, gorgeous bed and vintage roll-top bath. The Flamingo Room (201) is a deluxe double with an antique Chinese wardrobe and boho day-bed. We also liked the four newer rooms in The Stable (check out the original cast-iron hoist outside 301 and 302); 303 has a roll-top bath and big bay windows.

Hotel bar Venner Bar is named after a 17th-century highwayman, but today the only shots you'll hear are the ones being poured at the bar. On Friday evenings there are free canapés to kick off the weekend with. Last orders, 2am.

Hotel restaurant There are two. The main, neutral-toned restaurant is informal enough to make you feel as though you're dining at a friend's house – a friend who's extremely handy in the kitchen, mind. Marco Pierre White disciple Marc Montgomery's seafood-focused menu has netted press plaudits aplenty, and is on offer till 9.30pm. Out in the converted barn, the Stable is a less formal affair, with stone-baked pizzas, pies and 37 varieties of cider on offer.

Top table On fine days, outside in the former stableyard; on cold ones, by the fire.

Room service The full restaurant menu – plus anything bespoke that the chef can rustle up – is on offer during normal kitchen hours.

Dress code Vintage English weekend wear.

Local knowledge You're at the official Gateway to the Jurassic Coast; borrow the resident spaniels and go for a sea-breezy walk on the beach. Inland, follow the Brit Valley Way, which starts at West Bay.

LOCAL EATING AND DRINKING

Book a table for lunch or have a cream tea at the Hive Beach Café in Burton Bradstock, an alfresco favourite with award-winning ice-creams and smashing seafood (01308 897070). In West Bay, The Riverside Restaurant (01308 422011) serves up the very best fresh fish in a charming seasidey setting; you'll need a reservation. Bella's at 7 South Street in Bucky Doo Square serves delicious homemade cakes, soup and sandwiches. On Saturdays and during school holidays Bridport's Electric Palace provides family-friendly meals (01308 428354) although it's no longer the proper brasserie it once was.

GET A ROOM!

For more information, or to book this hotel, go to www.mrandmrssmith.com. Register your Smith membership card (see pages 4–5) to enjoy exclusive offers and privileges.

 SMITH MEMBER OFFER Free glass of champagne if you're eating in the restaurant.

The Bull Hotel 34 East Street, Bridport, Dorset DT6 3LF (01308 422878; www.thebullhotel.co.uk)

EAST SUSSEX

COASTLINE Downlands and shingly shores
COAST LIFE Tea shops and flip-flops

The East Sussex coast has always attracted crowds; in the height of summer, you may have to fight your way onto the beaches, just as the Romans and Normans once did. Despite its perennial bucket-and-spade appeal, the region – which for former resident Rudyard Kipling was 'beloved over all' – is also a realm of chalky downlands and tranquil villages, ideal for long walks followed by a congratulatory visit to a cosy country pub. The softness of the landscape is reflected in the quiet cobblestone charm of mediaeval market towns such as Rye, and in the creamy Regency façades and Victorian pleasure pursuits of Brighton. It's not all chocolate-box quaintness though; Sussex's proximity to the capital also gives the county a sharper, cultivated edge. Brighton in particular has a wealth of restaurants, clubs and cultural events worthy of its popularity with weekending urbanites.

GETTING THERE

Planes Gatwick (www.gatwickairport.com) is the best of the region's airports, 30 miles north of Brighton on the M23; the train takes half an hour. Heathrow and Luton are also handy, with fast transport connections.
Trains Brighton has extensive national rail links, with direct services to London Victoria, Reading, Bath and Bristol, among others. Take a high-speed train from St Pancras to Rye via Ashford in an hour and 10 minutes.
Automobiles Brighton can be reached via the M23, although parking can be costly and you don't need a car if you plan to stay anchored in the city. You'll want one to explore the more rural parts of East Sussex, though.

LOCAL KNOWLEDGE

Taxis Hail one of Brighton's fleet of blue-and-white hackney cabs on the street, go to a rank, or ring Streamline Taxis (01273 202020). In smaller towns, it's minicabs only; in Rye, try Taxi-Time (01797 224016).
Packing tips Most beaches are pebbly, so if you do like to be beside the seaside, bring some scuffable footwear and something to sit on – unless you want a permanently dimpled bottom.
Recommended reads Graham Greene's sinful novel *Brighton Rock*; historical satire *1066 and All That* by WC Sellar and RJ Yeatman; Rudyard Kipling's poetic *The Five Nations*.
Local specialities The region offers more besides seaside sticks of rock and candyfloss: Rye is celebrated for its

seafood, especially its scallops, and pure-bred Romney Marsh mutton is considered a delicacy. Also seek out cured meats and fish from the Weald Smokery; regional honey; and organic sausages from Boathouse Farm – you can pick them all up at Russells (01273 776789), a farm shop and deli in Hove. Sussex also produces some surprisingly good wines, including Loire-style whites from – don't snigger – Breaky Bottom vineyard (www.breakybottom.co.uk).
Perfect picnic The Devil's Dyke valley, in the South Downs just outside Brighton, is a beautiful spot commanding idyllic views over Sussex. The countryside around Rye offers romantic vistas over Romney Marsh; the long

golden beaches of Camber Sands are three miles from Rye, but locals recommend the quieter Winchelsea beach in the peak summer months.

And... For a fishy lunch on Brighton beach in summer, head to Jack & Linda's, a traditional fish-smoking shack on the seafront at King's Road Arches. You'll get addictive home-made fish soup and the best grilled-mackerel sandwiches imaginable; perfect with a squeeze of lemon.

WORTH GETTING OUT OF BED FOR

Viewpoint The white chalk cliffs of the beautiful Seven Sisters Country Park are best seen from Birling Gap, with fabulous vistas towards Beachy Head. Alternatively, scan your eyes across the Old Town of Hastings from the East Hill, home to Britain's steepest funicular.

Arts and culture A hot contender for the title of the UK's most flamboyant building, the Royal Brighton Pavilion was built for George IV and now houses the engaging Brighton Museum & Art Gallery (www.brighton.virtualmuseum.info). The Jerwood Gallery is a new addition to Hastings (www. jerwoodgallery.org) featuring abstract works from the early- to mid-20th century. Head to Great Dixter House and take a tour of their gardens (www.greatdixter.co.uk).

Activities Have a flutter on the dogs at Brighton's attractive greyhound track (www.brightondogs.co.uk), or on the horses at Brighton Racecourse (www. brighton-racecourse.co.uk). Head to the coast for water sports from windsurfing to powerboating; Lagoon Watersports (www.hovelagoon.co.uk) has excellent instructors and hire facilities in Brighton and Hove. Visit Sedlescombe Organic Wines near Battle, tour its pretty vineyard and taste the award-winning whites (www. englishorganicwine.co.uk). Alternatively, get your highs from the basket of a hot-air balloon (www.hotair.co.uk).

Daytripper Genteel seaside town Bexhill is looking lively these days: the De La Warr Pavilion is a Modernist masterpiece and houses an excellent contemporary arts centre (www.dlwp.com). Not lively enough? Take the 20-minute Lydd Air flight across the Channel (www. lyddair.com) – from the airport you can hop on a bicycle, ride into picturesque Le Touquet for lunch and be back for the afternoon flight to Rye. Don't forget your passport.

Children Bodiam Castle is a fairy-tale moated fortress near Robertsbridge; it will capture kids' imaginations. Child-friendly Drusillas Park in Alfriston (www.drusillas. co.uk) has penguins, meerkats and monkeys galore; Brighton's Sea Life centre is one of the best in the UK

(www.sealifeeurope.com). AA Milne based 100 Acre Wood in *Winnie-the-Pooh* on Ashdown Forest (www. ashdownforest.org); fans of the philosophical bear can still play Poohsticks on the original bridge and visit Pooh Corner in Hartfield.

Walks The 100-mile South Downs Way starts near Beachy Head and goes all the way to Winchester; the stretches near Brighton are among the most spectacular (www. nationaltrail.co.uk). The High Weald Landscape Trail and 1066 Walk both start at Rye; visit www.highweald. org for routes.

Shopping In Brighton, browse the boutiques and jewellery shops of the Lanes. Jeremy Hoye's twinkling emporium on Ship Street is a magpie's dream, with modern but elegant handmade pieces in platinum and gold (0845 094 3175). For artwork and homewares, we like Castor and Pollux down in King's Road Arches (01273 773776). Rye is the place to go for antiques and collectibles; Glass Etc on Rope Walk (01797 226600) is owned by the knowledgable expert and author Andy McConnell, and houses his amazing hoard of 20th-century glassware.

Something for nothing Ponder the origins of the Long Man of Wilmington – Europe's largest representation of the human form, which is scored into the northern flanks of the South Downs six miles north of Eastbourne.

Don't go home without... getting to Strand Quay in time to watch Rye's fishing fleet land its catch, as they do each morning. The quay also hosts Rye's excellent farmers' market every Wednesday.

EXCEPTIONALLY EAST SUSSEX

Neighbouring Kent may be top of the hops, but this county produces more than 60 excellent varieties of beer – so you'll need to be selective. Harveys in Lewes is the oldest brewery in the region, and is still the big local favourite. Try before you buy at its Brewery Shop on Cliffe High Street (www.harveys.org.uk), or do your sampling in one of the area's plentiful pubs.

DIARY

February Rye holds its Scallop Festival. May Hastings holds its bizarre Jack-in-the-Green Festival of Morris Dancing on May Day. Running 3–25 May, Brighton Festival is the biggest arts event in England, and includes the Brighton Festival Fringe (www.brightonfestival.org). May–August Glyndebourne Festival Opera is one of the year's top social fixtures (www. glyndebourne.com). July–August Gay Pride (www.brightonpride.org). September The Rye Festival is a long-established celebration of art and music (www.ryefestival.co.uk). November Lewes' Guy Fawkes celebrations are among the UK's finest.

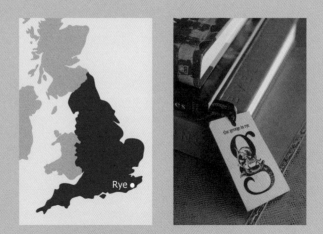

The George in Rye

STYLE Quirky-smart Regency inn
SETTING Cobbled Cinque Ports streets

'The ballroom's high walls are hung with a bird-patterned wallpaper; chairs clad in monochrome Florence Broadhurst textiles. It's decor that makes for love at first sight'

didn't mind. But the poor disbelieving Shakespeare-lookalike barman-cum-bag-wallah nearly herniated himself with Mrs Smith's make-up and a year's supply of fluorescent lycra.

The first thing we noticed about this 18th-century coaching inn was that the new owners seem to have achieved what few proprietors of these ancient public houses up and down the country have: a modern, redesigned interior that is still sympathetic to the original character of the building. It's not just that the black tar-encrusted beams have all been sand-blasted clean, or that the sticky red paisley carpets have given way to the original flagstone tiles. It's that no detail, from the nickel-coated plug sockets to burnished copper radiators, has been overlooked. Tightly packed with long sofas, chairs and beams, the George rises above the seagull-echoing street in a warren of little floors. Our room is extremely light and well planned, rendering it utterly inviting, helped in no small way by soft-touch scented pillows and hot-water bottle cosies. The bathroom has a Victorian-style bath/shower and is Ren-product equipped, while soft-blue wood panelling lends a gently nautical air. As soon as she opened the 'G'-branded wooden box to find an incredibly varied selection of teas, Mrs Smith immediately set to work preparing that most British of refreshments in celebration.

The owners, Katie and Alex Clarke, have links with set design and prop buying, making for a tasteful but vibrant and diverse decorative scheme: psychedelic Beatles prints sit alongside pockmarked beams and distressed leather. On our way to dinner, we nosed our way into the beautiful airy ballroom as it was being prepared for a wedding. The high walls are hung with a diverting bird-pattened wallpaper, and the chairs are clad in monochrome Florence Broadhurst textiles. It's decor that makes for love-at-first-sight stuff.

The chef creates bold but well balanced flavours. Local produce is at the fore, and starters such as dressed crab and smoked duck are quite something. The wine we chose was an English pinot noir – what an extraordinary revelation. Having tasted no better Gevrey-Chambertin from Burgundy itself, it instantly became an all-time favourite.

We weren't the only ones feeling celebratory, don't forget. And, as many of the bedrooms lead straight to the ballroom's heavy doors, that night, as we climbed

Considering I'd just slipped a disc and had promised to cycle over the Alps the following Monday, our stay at the George in Rye needed to live up to expectations. That, or my pathetic squeals of pain would reverberate through their towel cupboards and kitchens and onwards to those very edelweiss gorges. Thankfully, the hotel has a reputation for being comfortable and traditional, yet stylish – thanks to being touched by the hand of film-set designers. Just what the doctor ordered.

Mrs Smith drove under an ancient fortified Old Town gate, dropped me outside the George, unloaded the bags and told the staff that on no account was I to carry anything. Humiliating verbal castration upon arrival. Great. While she searched for a (rare) parking space, my bag-heaving receptionist was very sweet. I asked if I could store my bike in the garage, which was of course fine. I tried to explain that cycling was good for my back, to assuage my guilt at the exercise/laziness contradiction. She really the stairs in a pleasant post-prandial daze, a growing din of wedding-reception disco filled us with dread. But, thanks to some extraordinarily good soundproofing, Mrs Smith, with her owl-standard hearing, was able to restrict her deadly talons' nocturnal tasks to clutching the crisp bedding.

Next morning, at a slobbish 10.30am, we took breakfast in our slightly small but excitingly bouncy bed. I went all full English; Mrs Smith purred as she lapped up home-made yogurt and raspberry compote. Later, while she pottered about Rye, buying fudge and millinery just up the High Street, I went for a cycle, and found the landscape around Rye flat, windy and abundant in sheep. I attempted to ride along Camber Sands, but couldn't. I sank. Children laughed at me; adults pointed. But the incredible light on the beach, glistening on sand and glittering on waves, made up for my public humiliation.

Having wound my lycra'd way back through bobbing poppies and pea fields stretching into the horizon, I was looking forward to bar snacks and bitter. A superb lamb burger, sticky caramelised chunky chips and a fresh local pint did the

'Psychedelic Beatles prints sit alongside pockmarked beams and distressed leather'

trick, and I happily read the papers on the enclosed, decked courtyard of the George. Luckily, no one appeared to derive too much amusement from my hairless thighs.

Smiles were more forthcoming during our visit to the nearby pampering palace, the Rye Retreat, however, where Mrs Smith had booked me in for a full-body massage and facial. Having only read of such things in sneaked teenage glances through mum's *Cosmo*, I was a tad nervous, and desperate to let all the nice ladies know that I fancied girls. They didn't seem to care, and Karen, my masseur and face-scrubber, soon put me at ease. I came out smelling of tangerines and lemon sorbet. The back was in a dreamy state and Mrs Smith was warbling something about fantastic bum toners; life was pretty good.

Rye – you made converts of us. OK, this East Sussex spot may present more-than-ample kitsch bric-a-brac window-sniggering opportunities, and maybe its one-way system is a little annoying to first-time users, but the charm and romance of this ancient fishing town is undeniable. And, if it is trying to shrug off its unfair bucket-and-spade image, then the George in Rye will help its cause no end. And as for my slipped disc – well, our weekend worked a treat on that, too.

Reviewed by Nick Hussey

NEED TO KNOW

Rooms 24 (with 10 more in the pipeline), including junior suites.

Rates £135–£295, including breakfast. Bookings for a one-night stay on Saturdays incur a £50 supplement.

Check-out 11.30am (but flexible on request).

Facilities Courtyard garden, DVD library, private dining and screening room, in-room spa treatments, free WiFi, bike hire. In rooms, flatscreen TV, Vi-Spring bed, Frette linens, marble-edged (or roll-top) bath, rain shower head, Ren toiletries.

Children Welcome. An extra bed (£20) or cot (£10) can be added to rooms, along with baby essentials including a changing mat, wet wipes, nappies – and a rubber duck.

Also Lavender-filled pillows and luxurious bottles of wild fig oil imported from Florence make evenings-in even more relaxing.

IN THE KNOW

Our favourite rooms Each room is unique, so you're bound to have your own preference, but we like cosy, pretty room 3; room 10 in the eaves with a roll-top bath; and elegantly decorated room 2. Room 6 has a gorgeous shower stall made from a wig cupboard. For a special weekend, book suite 1 for its double-headed walk-in shower.

Hotel bar Sip on a Rye Smile whiskey cocktail or glass of Sussex wine amid the George Tap's attractive mish-mash of wooden tables, benches and chairs; it stays open until the last guest leaves.

Hotel restaurant The brasserie-style Dining Room has been expanded with Paul Gordon (who won acclaim at Qualia in Australia) the head chef responsible for the hotel's traditional English cuisine using local and seasonal ingredients.

Top table Nestle in a corner at either end of the long banquette, or outside in the Garden Courtyard on balmy evenings.

Room service Light snacks available 24 hours; from 7am to 10pm, you can order from the restaurant's menu.

Dress code Laid-back layers; something a little smarter for dinner.

Local knowledge Browse the antiques shops along the Strand Quay, or stroll down to gorgeous Camber Sands with a bulging picnic hamper packed for you by the George.

LOCAL EATING AND DRINKING

There's no shortage of cafés and tearooms in Rye, but you'll be magnetically drawn to the cream cakes and savoury temptations at Fletchers House on Lion Street (01797 222227). Just outside the town's mediaeval gate, Landgate Bistro has an excellent menu of classic and contemporary British dishes (01797 222829). Have a meal at The Ship Inn (01797 222233) at the bottom of Mermaid Street. The menu champions local, seasonal ingredients, with dishes ranging from the traditional (potted shrimp with potato and thyme bread) to the unexpected (grilled sea trout with sushi rice, pickled vegetables and avocado). Rye might seem an unusual spot to find authentic Italian, but The Tuscan Kitchen (01797 223269) on Lion Street is run by a husband-and-wife team, and ingredients are plucked from their farm in Italy.

GET A ROOM!

For more information, or to book this hotel, go to www.mrandmrssmith.com. Register your Smith membership card (see pages 4–5) to enjoy exclusive offers and privileges.

Smith SMITH MEMBER OFFER A seasonal pre-dinner cocktail each in the bar or restaurant.

The George in Rye 98 High Street, Rye, East Sussex TN31 7JT (01797 222114; www.thegeorgeinrye.com)

Square

STYLE Fresh-faced townhouse
SETTING Brightonian Regency square

'Metropolitan refugees can grab a
dose of sea air without having to forgo
life's essentials: billowing duvets,
properly made mojitos'

Brighton is where London traditionally dangles its legs in the sea. It's a jaunty bastion of the dirty weekend, an unflinching champion of end-of-the-pier frivolity, a gay-welcoming resort where no one's too old to have fun and even the seagulls have attitude. An ideal place, then, for Mr and Mrs Smith to enjoy some old-fashioned decadence by the pounding waves.

We arrive by train in just 50 minutes. Being so close to the capital, Brighton has long been the perfect escape for urbanites who want to get away but can't face anything as tiresome as a long drive, airport security, or, heaven forbid, countryside mud. Its best hotels know this, and have developed a style-savvy individuality that ensures metropolitan refugees can grab a healthy dose of sea air at this low-key abode without having to forgo life's little essentials: billowing duvets and properly made mojitos.

Kitted out in its best whites, Square follows this brief to a designer T. With just 10 rooms, it occupies five floors of a slender townhouse overlooking a small park, and is set amid the liberated streets of Kemp Town. Brighton Pier and the long, breezy seafront lie just round the corner, while key shops and sights are just a wander away.

Square, naturally enough, is not at all square. There's no nameplate, and its clean, contemporary interiors offer a harmonious mix of white furniture, greenish glass and shiny wooden floors in various shades of toast. This minimalism extends to staffing levels – a lone host meets, greets and mixes drinks for us, and our fellow guests, who are all well-mannered twosomes, gay and straight. The service is relaxed and attentive, but if you're the sort of party animal who likes a hangover-beating fry-up the next morning, note that Square has no restaurant or room-service menu. Breakfast is a bountiful spread of summer fruits, yoghurts, bagels and pecan-and-sultana toast, served with good coffee in an arty lounge that, at night, gets transformed into a ritzy cocktail bar with jazzy sounds. Fond of a Sunday morning lie-in, we ask for breakfast to be delivered to our room with *The Observer*, and so it all comes – bang on time, with a smile.

This being Britain, and a bank holiday weekend, it is of course raining. Fortunately, we've booked the 'reverse penthouse', which offers loft-style living in an airy

basement stretching the length of the building. It comes with a trendy gas fire, glistening kitchen, mighty flatscreen TV, lots of dimmer switches and a super-comfy bed graced with creamy throws and cushions in faux polar bear skin. We've arranged to see some old friends, who pop round to look suitably impressed and enjoy a bottle of champagne that's been chilling in the fridge – Square's welcome gift to holders of the Mr & Mrs Smith membership card.

'Brighton's all about eating and shopping,' our long-lost chums explain, and advise booking restaurants well in advance. We walk to Blanch House, another townhouse that's metamorphosed into a hotel. Their bar's cocktail list is so long you immediately think: 'Crikey, I need a cocktail to look at this...' Having been disco-dancing until 2am the

previous night, Mrs Smith orders a reviving Posh Gringo (chilli-infused tequila, ginger, lime, champagne), then romps through a dinner of quail, monkfish and rhubarb crumble. The dining room is another artfully whitewashed basement, its tables packed with couples served by staff who may well give you a kiss on departure.

The next morning, we clear our heads with a walk on the pier, which is a commendably tacky parade of fortune-tellers, scary rides, fairground stalls and teeth-rotting treats. Don't worry, high culture is also available in the visual extravaganza that is the Royal Pavilion, which, after sex, must surely be voted the next best reason to come here. Decorated with a wild, budget-blowing splendour, this Orientalist, 1815 palace is a flamboyant reminder that, in Brighton, permission to party comes by royal appointment.

With the weather unremittingly soggy, our will to shop is tempered by the irresistible pull of the pub – though we see enough to realise that if you want to pick up a tattoo, Danish lamp, organic turnip or some hot new art, Brighton's the place. Antiques and established names congregate in the historic Lanes, including the fabulous jeweller Jeremy Hoye; while North Laine has quirkier one-off shops, such as colourful tailors Gresham Blake.

Having had our designer fill, we settle down in the Heart and Hand, a refreshingly unyuppified pub that serves the local Harveys ale and has an heirloom Rock-Ola jukebox from which Hendrix and Springfield still belt it out. A couple of pints later, we move on to lunch at Bill's, which is like a mad vegetable garden filled with pine tables. You can't book, but it's worth queuing for the terrific salads, soups and sandwiches. Then, at the Hotel du Vin, drinking Ardbeg malt whisky, we reflect on how Brighton really does bring out the debauchery in one. 'I think I need a little lie-down,' Mrs Smith sighs, an idea Mr Smith has always approved of. So we head back to Square to light the fire, pull down the blinds and, er, have a cup of tea.

Reviewed by Nigel Tisdall

'Enjoy some old-fashioned decadence by the pounding waves'

NEED TO KNOW

Rooms Nine, plus a 'reverse penthouse' apartment in the basement.

Rates Sunday to Thursday, £85–£245; weekend, £135–£380, including Continental breakfast.

Check-out 11am, but will try to accommodate advance requests for later times. Check-in, 3pm–9.30pm.

Facilities DVD library, free WiFi throughout, beauty treatments and massages can be arranged. In rooms, flatscreen LCD TV, DVD/CD player, minibar, tea/coffee, Molton Brown toiletries.

Children This playpen is strictly for the grown-ups.

Also No pets allowed. There's a two-night minimum stay at weekends; over New Year, a three-night minimum stay is required from 31 December to 2 January. The hotel is closed Christmas Eve and on Christmas Day.

IN THE KNOW

Our favourite rooms King rooms 3, 5 and 7 enjoy sea views and free-standing Philippe Starck baths; glass walls allow you to see the surf while you bathe. The hotel's pièce de résistance is a large, decadent penthouse, unexpectedly located in the basement; it has a Jacuzzi bath and open fireplace.

Hotel bar There is a stylish cocktail bar, open until midnight, with crystal chandeliers, white leather sofas and cubic stools, and a relaxed, jazzy soundtrack.

Hotel restaurant There's no restaurant, but Brighton is blessed with a range of good eating-out options. Breakfast is served in the bar from 8am–9.30am on weekdays, 9am–10.30am at weekends.

Top table Next to the fireplace or on the banquette-style sofa in the bay-window recess.

Room service Drinks and breakfast can be delivered to your boudoir until midday.

Dress code Anything goes, but you might want to smarten up in the evening, or you'll feel scruffy against all those sleek white lines in the bar.

Local knowledge The Lanes is an excellent place for a wander, with lots of little jewellery shops, antiques showrooms and designer boutiques to browse. Gresham Blake on Bond Street in the North Laine area does a particularly fine line in natty gents' attire and bespoke tailoring (01273 609587; www.greshamblake.com); stop off for a coffee in Brighton Square.

LOCAL EATING AND DRINKING

Wash down some boiled organic eggs and thick-cut soldiers with a Bloody Mary, or have a hearty steak sandwich and a glass of wine at Bill's Produce Store, a deli-cum-café meets organic greengrocer on North Road (01273 692894). In Kings Arches, Due South is a fantastic seafront restaurant, with organic and bio-dynamic wines and a seasonal menu of Sussex's best produce (01273 821218). Seven Dials on Buckingham Place (01273 885555) has a seasonal menu that rotates every six weeks. Hotel du Vin on Ship Street (01273 718588) has an acclaimed French bistro, helpful sommeliers, and a well-stocked bar. Boutique hotel Blanch House on Atlingworth Street (01273 603504) has an intimate restaurant, with seasonal à la carte and tasting menus, and a chic cocktail bar. Roast breast of pheasant, baked stuffing and parsnip puree is just one of the culinary delights to be found on The Ginger Dog's hearty menu, a modern gastro-pub on College Place (01273 620990). Classic and novel fish dishes meet at Riddle and Fins, the champagne and oyster bar whose menu is bursting with flavour and flair on Meeting House Lane (01273 323008).

GET A ROOM!

For more information, or to book this hotel, go to www.mrandmrssmith.com. Register your Smith membership card (see pages 4–5) to enjoy exclusive offers and privileges.

 SMITH MEMBER OFFER A bottle of champagne on arrival; let the hotel know your ETA in advance, to ensure it's perfectly chilled when you get there.

Square 4 New Steine, Brighton BN2 1BP (01273 691777; www.squarebrighton.com)

HAMPSHIRE

COUNTRYSIDE Forests, farms and market towns
COUNTRY LIFE Rural road trips, sea-view strolls

A hop from London, Hampshire has long been the go-to county for green and pleasant getaways. What could be more picturesque than New Forest ponies roaming through filmic glades like a Disney dream sequence? Perhaps it's the pastoral patchwork of farm and field, the traditional charm of biscuit-box villages or just the promise of a great pub lunch that make this area so alluring, but beyond the county's rustic-idyll clichés, there are plenty of up-tempo enticements on offer. Portsmouth's nautical glories are a must for naval gazers (ahem); and Farnborough's aviation hub promises spectacular sky larks. If you'd rather keep your feet on the ground (or on the pedals, or in the stirrups), explore William the Conqueror's hunting spot of choice: the vast New Forest. This is a land of country drives in leafy lanes, picnic lunches on grassy hilltops and scouting for vintage finds at antiques fairs: it's life at its leisurely best.

GETTING THERE

Planes Gatwick and Heathrow are the county's major international gateways, but Bournemouth (www.bournemouthairport.com) and Southampton (www.southamptonairport.com) are better placed if you're hitting the coast or the New Forest.

Trains Southern and South West Trains link London Waterloo to major cities such as Portsmouth, Southampton and Winchester, as well as smaller towns such as New Milton. Short distances from town to town make rail travel an easy, eco-friendly option (www.nationalrail.co.uk).

Automobiles Hampshire's tree-lined lanes and forest roads are perfect for old-school rural road trips, with plenty of village-pub stop-offs and ooh-let's-go-see-that detours.

LOCAL KNOWLEDGE

Taxis You're better off booking ahead in smaller towns. Brockenhurst Taxis (01425 619922) are handy for getting around the New Forest area and Southampton Taxis (023 8039 2798) cover the city and surroundings pretty well.

Packing tips An open-top and driving goggles/Hepburn headscarves for classic countryside jaunts; a rambler's cane for New Forest wanderings.

Recommended reads Pack your classics: Jane Austen spent most of her life here – *Pride and Prejudice* and *Sense and Sensibility* both take inspiration from the area. Anthony Trollope's *Barchester Towers* is set in a fictional Winchester and virtually everything penned by Thomas Hardy takes place in Wessex – the ancient kingdom of which Hampshire comprised a hefty chunk.

Local specialities Farm products – sausages, cheeses and ice-creams – figure high on the agenda, and the River Test's trout have kept local smokeries in business for centuries. New Forest venison is particularly prized; try it and its feathery game counterparts at Blackmoor Game (www.blackmoorgame.co.uk) near New Alresford. Salad fans, note, Hampshire is the UK's watercress heartland.

Perfect picnic If you don't fancy pick 'n' mixing from farmers' markets and delis, make a beeline for the Vanilla Pod café in Lymington (01590 673828), which will put together a picnic if you give them a call a day before. Set out for the Rhinefield Ornamental Drive near Brockenhurst. Park at Blackwater carpark and locate a spot among the azaleas and rhododendrons (at their resplendent best in May and June).

And... Born-and-bred Hampshire locals have borne the unflattering nickname 'Hampshire Hogs' for centuries. According to 18th-century lexicographer Frances Grose, it is a 'jocular appellation for a Hampshire man; Hampshire being famous for a fine breed of hogs, and the excellency of the bacon made there.' The county is still justifiably proud of its pork products – apparently the New Forest acorns make for particularly flavoursome sausages.

WORTH GETTING OUT OF BED FOR

Viewpoint Ramble the North Hampshire Downs and make the meandering ascent up Pilot Hill, the highest point in the county. From the top, you can look down across a pastoral patchwork of grassland and woods over into neighbouring Berkshire.

Arts and culture Portsmouth is mother city of the Royal Navy, and it really won't let you forget it. HMS *Victory*, HMS *Warrior* and the *Mary Rose* loom large in the harbour, and the waterfront is lined with museums devoted to nautical warfare. Literary landlubbers can visit Charles Dickens' birthplace which houses the sofa on which the author met his maker (www. charlesdickensbirthplace.co.uk), or leave town for Chawton to scout out Jane Austen's house, where she worked on almost all her major novels on a tiny writing table (www.jane-austens-house-museum.org.uk).

Activities You can bob along in the basket of a hot-air balloon – champagne in hand – with Adventure Balloons (www.adventureballoons.co.uk). Hone your polo skills at Brett Polo (www.brettpolo.com) in Winkfield, or get saddle-sore exploring the New Forest by bike (www. cyclex.co.uk) or on horseback (www.burleyvilla.co.uk). In Farnborough, the Cabair Flying School will happily plonk you in the cockpit of a small plane or helicopter and send you to the skies (www.cabairflyingschools.com).

Daytripper The serene slice of yesteryear that is the Isle of Wight sits two miles off the Hampshire coast and is easily reached by car ferry from Portsmouth to Ryde (www.wightlink.com) and also from Southampton to Cowes (www.redfunnel.co.uk) – ferries run every half-hour or so. Once landed, head over to the Victorian fishing town of Ventnor for coastal walks, lighthouse spotting and pub lunches. Unleash the kids at the isle's fêted fun park, Blackgang Chine, on the south-west coast (www.blackgangchine.com).

Children Introduce young Smiths to Ralph, the wetsuited penguin at Marwell Wildlife near Winchester (his feathers fell off; the suit saves him from sunburn). The park is also home to around 250 species from all over the globe, including tigers, crocs, giraffes and snow leopards (www.marwell.org.uk). For more aquatic animal antics, Portsmouth's Blue Reef Aquarium is one of the UK's best sea-life centres (www.bluereefaquarium.co.uk).

Walks The New Forest is riddled with walking trails. There's a lovely circular route from the village of Lyndhurst through the outlying hamlets of Pikes Hill, Emery Down and Swann Green that doubles as a mini country pub crawl, taking in thatched cottages, pretty churches and, naturally, glorious Hampshire countryside.

Shopping Portsmouth and Southampton see to any high-street needs, and Basingstoke's Festival Place is one for the mallrats – although it does host a farmers' market every Saturday, too (www.festivalplace.co.uk). Hampshire is heaven for antique-hunters, with dozens of shops selling furniture and bric-a-brac dotted all over the county. Gaylords in Titchfield has a remarkable stock of vintage furniture (www.gaylords.co.uk).

Something for nothing OK, so it's not King Arthur's actual Round Table that currently resides in Winchester's atmospheric Great Hall, but the 14th-century forgery – painted for Henry VIII – still merits a look-see (www.hants.gov.uk/greathall).

Don't go home without... ascending the Spinnaker Tower. From the crow's-nest of the 170-metre edifice in Portsmouth Harbour you can see 23 miles out to sea.

HAPPILY HAMPSHIRE

The New Forest has enjoyed privileged status since William the Conqueror realised its native deer were rather tasty and legally preserved the land for royal hunting jaunts. For the thousand-odd years since his decree, a large part of the forest (and its population of 3,000 wild ponies) has been looked after by verderers (landowners also known as 'commoners' – but in a nice way) and five elected agisters, who manage the land and its livestock.

DIARY

July Eyes turn skywards every even year, for the Farnborough International Airshow where the aerospace industry goes to town, with astonishing feats of flying, including the Red Arrows (www.farnborough.com). The Hampshire Food Festival celebrates all things edible, with events throughout the county including sausage-making lessons, brewery tours, bee-keeping events and cookery classes (www.hampshirefare.co.uk/food-festival). **August** Every year since 1826, the Solent has swarmed with sailors, pitting their vessels against each other for Cowes Week, the world's longest running regatta, culminating in a spectacular firework display (www.cowesweek.co.uk).

Lyndhurst

Lime Wood

STYLE Mannered modern manor
SETTING New Forest's ancient capital

'The kind of place to spend your bonus admiring a beautiful view, pretending to be country types, without leaving your freestanding bath'

bonus admiring a beautiful view, pretending to be country types, without leaving your freestanding bath. Lime Wood's setting is magnificent, and the building was impressive even before extensive remodelling added a fabulous central atrium with a retractable roof.

Imaginative annexes have been added to the 29-bedroom property, and an enormous spa, more Champneys than Chiva Som, is set to be booked solid by locals. The gardens are not yet mature, but already spectacular, and showcase excellent sculptures. Inside, David Collins' decor has won awards, and is what I'd describe as Hotel Costes meets Daylesford: lots of silk upholstery in cool subdued Farrow & Ball shades and rustic touches applied with exquisite taste. There's even a basement billiard room with cigars and a massive screen for Sky Sports. The place simply reeks of cash.

And here we are, the Derham family, with our mismatched luggage, too-cool 10-year-old tomboy and hot-pant-wearing four-year-old, alongside my exuberant entrepreneur Mr Smith. 'This isn't a business venture, this is a trophy asset,' he decrees in less-than-subtle tones as we're shown to our quarters. Is it a little house? A maisonette? Or a duplex? I'm not sure of terminology to suit such rarified surroundings, but there's a rather lovely sitting room with a massive sofa bed for the girls, French windows opening onto our own terrace, and the forest beyond. Upstairs, an opulent master suite displays an orgy of cushions on the bed and the bathroom's array of fluffy towels is just as extravagant.

The next morning, I declare our little corner of Lime Wood 'New England show home' in look. White painted slatted walls, exposed eaves, sisal matting, everything gleaming, no detail overlooked. (Actually, they forgot a corkscrew, but the nice tweed-capped chap soon puts that right.) There's even fresh fruit and reference books full of tips on identifying the native trees and on how to forage for mushrooms. Yes, there are two massive plasma TVs, but the kids are champing at the bit to choose from a rainbow of borrowable Hunter wellies and bikes. As there are not yet child seats or stabilisers, Mr Smith rediscovers the lost art of the 'backie' and we're off.

Enid Blyton would be proud if she could see us pedalling away in the sun, our cheery faces glowing as we explore

S potting wild ponies and singing loudly to the *Glee* soundtrack in glorious evening sunshine isn't a *bad* way to pass the time in the mother of all traffic jams. But this is to be expected on a Friday evening, on the road into Lyndhurst. Despite the plodding pace, it is with peckers up that we turn off the Beaulieu Road to Lime Wood. In the style of all proper country-house arrivals, we approach a suitably patrician Georgian house in golden stone along a sweeping drive flanked by well-tended lawns. Perfection. All we need is a dashingly handsome young man in a slightly self-conscious tweed cap to take our bags. Ah yes, there he is. Next, cheery front-of-housers joke with the children, ignoring chocolatey faces and bare feet. Lime Wood, you do welcomes very well indeed.

The new owners have spent five years and untold millions creating a destination that offers the last word in out-of-town indulgence. The kind of place to spend your cycle paths galore. A corner of England where sturdy ponies with fluffy ankles roam freely is undeniably special, especially when you can cycle energetically and safely down country lanes.

Later, in the sepia tint of this uncharacteristically clement spring weather, we turn back the clock to 1950, and go crab fishing on Mudeford Quay. Next thing, we're riding horses through the kind of ancient forest that Robin and his merry men would have happily capered about in. How comforting to know that, should the heavens open, we could head back to Lime Wood, settle back against the scatter cushions, book a massage, and order tip-top room service.

Mealtimes are when hotels show their mettle, never more so than when they sell themselves as luxury hotels that actively welcome children. This isn't a nursery tea and babysitters kind of place (though they are available); this is a grown-up environment that is genuinely friendly towards kids. It's a tricky path to navigate, and I heartily applaud any establishment that succeeds. There are two restaurants – the Scullery, for fantastic breakfasts, lunches and relaxed suppers, and also a full-on posh-crockery formal dining room – and, unusually, kids are welcome at both.

'I declare our little corner 'New England show home' in look... Slatted walls, exposed eaves, everything gleaming'

Dithering over world-class cocktails in the atrium, we munch on olives as big as the gobstoppers in Lyndhurst's Ye Olde Sweet Shoppe. Confronted by the all-adult, well-dressed clientele in the smart Dining Room restaurant, we consider a stage-left exit to the Scullery. Yet, feeling it our duty to you, dear Mr & Mrs Smith reader, to sample that tasting menu, we stay committed. Yes, we're going Michelin-starred all for you. At this point we meet Lime Wood's charming Belgian maître d'. Proffering top-drawer amuse-bouches, he suggests that our family might like the best spot in the hotel: seats at the chef's table in the kitchen – a rare privilege, of course – plus the best of the menus, accompanied by the theatre of watching the chefs at work. It is a masterstroke of diplomacy and bonhomie.

There's no question that Lime Wood is a hotel prepared to go to any length to ensure its guests, whatever age, get what they want. It's not what you'd call understated, and neither – having counted the Porsches and Ferraris in the car park – are its guests. But Lime Wood delivers on its promise of luxury, with genuine friendliness, and damn-fine melon martinis. Welcome, ladies and gents, to the Nouveau Forêt.

Reviewed by Katie Derham

NEED TO KNOW

Rooms 29, including 15 suites.

Rates £245–£750, not including breakfast (around £10 for Continental; £15 for full English).

Check-out Midday, but flexible, subject to availability. Earliest check-in, 3pm.

Facilities Library of books and DVDs, pool, snooker and billiards, mountain bikes and wellies for guests, walking and running trails, valet parking, helipad, free WiFi throughout. Herb House Spa has an indoor pool. In rooms: flatscreen TV, CD/DVD player, preloaded iPod, free bottled water and Bamford bath products.

Children Little Smiths are well looked after at Lime Wood: extra beds and cots are free, there's a children's menu, and bikes and scooters to borrow. Babysitting with a local nanny costs £45 for four hours (48 hours' notice required).

Also Pets are allowed in the outside lodgings – the Coach House, Crescent and Pavilions. In-room spa and beauty treatments can be arranged.

IN THE KNOW

Our favourite rooms For honeymoon-perfect privacy, go for Pavilion 1 – it's separate from the main house and has a dramatic black vaulted ceiling, four-poster bed and a roll-top bath in an alcove overlooking the green pastures outside. The bedrooms in the main house are also high on romance, thanks mainly to the elegant Italian marble bathrooms in soft grey and white – Rooms 1 and 2 have bath tubs beneath wide sash windows, and Room 11 has double sinks and an enormous bathroom. If you like a quirky attic abode, plump for an Eaves room.

Hotel bar Max's Bar is a relaxed, sophisticated spot, manned by Max himself – a Sicilian barman who has expertly mixed drinks since he helped out in his dad's watering hole as a child.

Hotel restaurant The whitewashed Scullery is bright, cheery, and best for a casual lunch or dinner. You can sometimes catch a hog roasting in the fireplace. The Dining Room is more formal, with yellow lamps on carved chandeliers, ash-panelled walls, snug banquettes and a rarefied British menu. Chef Luke Holder is a fan of locally sourced ingredients: the meat is hand-reared on Lime Wood land and the fungi are foraged from neighbouring woods.

Top table Pick a quiet table for two by the window, or ask to dine at the chef's table in the kitchen.

Room service An excerpt of the Scullery menu is on offer 24 hours a day.

Dress code There's a grown-up manor feel, so clean off the country muck before dinner.

Local knowledge Let Lime Wood know in advance and the hotel will arrange a kayak trip on the nearby Beaulieu River. Visit the vintage cars at the Motor Museum in Beaulieu, then walk along the river to Bucklers Hard (lovely at high tide).

LOCAL EATING AND DRINKING

At Beaulieu, call in at The Master Builder's at Bucklers Hard (01590 616253) for lunch or dinner – this elegant rustic pub makes the most of the excellent local produce, turning a recent shoot's venison into sausages and cooking up comforting Sunday roasts. More locally sourced fare awaits at The Oak Inn on Pinkney Lane in Bank (023 8028 2350) – seafood from Lymington in summer and game from within a five-mile radius in winter. For something more Continental, head to Franoi on the high street in Lyndhurst (023 8028 3745), an Italian trattoria serving up authentic delights from Emilia Romagna.

GET A ROOM!

For more information, or to book this hotel, go to www.mrandmrssmith.com. Register your Smith membership card (see pages 4–5) to enjoy exclusive offers and privileges.

 SMITH MEMBER OFFER A bottle of house red or white if you book an Eaves, Cosy, Spacious or Generous room; a bottle of champagne with the Forest , Forest Hideaway or Pavilion Suites.

Lime Wood Beaulieu Road, Lyndhurst, Hampshire SO43 7FZ (023 8028 7177; www.limewood.co.uk)

LIVERPOOL

CITYSCAPE Revitalised Victoriana
CITY STYLE Mersey beat

This stately old lady on the banks of the Mersey may have celebrated her 800th birthday, but there's plenty of life in the old girl yet: she's enjoying an invigorating shake-up that shines a flattering spotlight on her Victorian splendours and spruced-up docksides. The World Heritage site not only has Europe's oldest Chinatown and the UK's largest cathedral, but it is also a former European Capital of Culture. Liverpool's irrepressible cheeriness has been combined with a renaissance in art and culture not seen since the Fab Four took an unsuspecting world by storm back in the Sixties. The city once famous for its maritime prowess and musical clout has reclaimed its wharves and warehouses, transforming them into enticing café and museum districts, and fresh blood pulses through Liverpool's grand Imperial arteries and neoclassical structures, where buzzing restaurants, boutiques and nightlife now hold sway.

GETTING THERE

Planes Liverpool John Lennon Airport (www.liverpool airport.com) is about eight miles south of the city centre and offers regular services to London and Europe. An express bus operates to Liverpool city centre and Lime Street railway station.

Trains Intercity services arrive at Lime Street station; ring National Rail Enquiries (0845 748 4950) for details.

Automobiles By motorway, you'll approach Liverpool on the M62, M53 or M58. The journey from London via the M6 takes between four and five hours; from Birmingham, it's less than two. Liverpool is well connected by bus; the main stations are at Paradise Street and Queen Square.

Boats Gerry and the Pacemakers have a lot to answer for; you can see the city from the ferry across the Mersey, or cruise the Manchester Ship Canal with Mersey Ferries (www.merseyferries.co.uk).

LOCAL KNOWLEDGE

Taxis There are plenty of black cabs in Liverpool, especially in the city centre; just hail one in the street. Alternatively, try Mersey Cabs (0151 298 2222).

Packing tips Load up your iPod with your favourite tunes, from Merseybeat to cosmic Scouse (aka the Zutons, the La's, the Dead 60s and the Coral, to name a few).

Recommended reads Collected Poems by Roger McGough; Love Poems by Brian Patten; Beryl Bainbridge's An Awfully Big Adventure is a bittersweet study of the city in the Fifties; Tony Quinn's The Rescue Man.

Local specialities Try a scouse – a hearty lamb and vegetable stew – or a wet nelly, a syrup-soaked pudding made from cake and pastry scraps. The monthly Lark Lane Farmers' Market (0151 233 2165) features produce from within a 100-mile radius, incorporating the rich surrounding farmland of Lancashire and Cheshire. Track down HS Bourne's handmade organic Cheshire cheeses (www.hsbourne.co.uk), and delicious smoked meats from the Port of Lancaster Smokehouse (www.polsco.co.uk).

Perfect picnic The grand country estate of Croxteth Hall (www.croxteth.co.uk) just to the north of the city is flanked by 500 acres of beautiful parkland, with woodland walks and riding stables. Bring a blanket and find a quiet spot, or sprawl supine on the lawns of the walled garden.

WORTH GETTING OUT OF BED FOR

Viewpoint Standing 101 metres tall, Liverpool Cathedral's Vestey Tower (www.liverpoolcathedral.org.uk) offers panoramic vistas across the city, reaching as far as the Welsh hills to the west and Pennines to the east. You'll have to take two lifts up to the bell tower housing the 14.5-ton Great George bell, then climb 108 stairs to the viewing platform. Ring 0151 709 6271 for visiting hours.

Arts and culture As one might expect from an ex-European Capital of Culture, Liverpool has some of the country's best art galleries; the Walker Art Gallery (www.thewalker.org.uk) has works by Rembrandt, Freud and Hockney. In a beautifully converted Albert Dock warehouse, Tate Liverpool (www.tate.org.uk) has an excellent collection of modern and contemporary art. For a round-up of other cultural stars in town, visit www.liverpoolmuseums.org.uk.

Activities In this football-mad city you're either red or blue (or Tranmere Rovers); you can see Liverpool in action at Anfield (www.liverpoolfc.tv), and Everton at Goodison Park (www.evertonfc.com) – just make sure you wear the right colours. Just north of Liverpool is the Aintree racecourse, home of the Grand National, but the course hosts plenty of other race events throughout the year (www.aintree.co.uk). If you prefer to be in the saddle yourself, you can take lessons at Croxteth Park Riding Centre (0151 220 9177).

Daytripper The Sefton Coastal Path stretches for a little over 12 miles between the seaside resorts of Crosby and Southport, taking in beaches, dunes, woodlands and nature reserves for red squirrels and rare toads. Crosby beach is populated by Antony Gormley's eerie army of cast-iron men, collectively known as *Another Place*. Merseyrail Northern Line trains stop at every town along the coast from Liverpool to Southport, so you can walk as little or as far as you like. Cut out the boring bits with a guide from Sefton Tourism (01704 533533).

Children The Yellow Duckmarine offers trips in a WWII amphibious truck. The hour-long tour takes in the historic sights of the city (Pier Head, the Three Graces, St George's Hall, cathedrals etc), before splashing down in the Salthouse Dock, ending at Albert Dock. Drivers carry water pistols for kids to shoot at passers-by (www.theyellowduckmarine.co.uk). The Walker Art Gallery (www.thewalker.org.uk) on William Brown Street is home to the first dedicated children's gallery in any UK museum; Big Art for Little Artists offers hands-on painting sessions and child-friendly activities.

Just down the road is the huge World Museum Liverpool (www.liverpoolmuseums.org.uk), with interactive displays on classic childhood fetishes from dinosaurs and Egyptian mummies to space travel. Acorn Venture Urban Farm (www.acornfarm.co.uk) on Knowsley Industrial Estate has a petting zoo, plus pony rides and a farm shop.

Walks From Seacombe Ferry Terminal, take a bracing stroll alongside the river Mersey and the Irish Sea: follow the promenade round to West Kirby via New Brighton (where there's a rail link back to Seacombe, if the full 15 miles will spoil your lunch plans).

Shopping There are enough designer outlets to satisfy any WAG. Flannels at the Met Quarter (www.metquarter.com) stocks lines by Italy's own fab four (Prada, Dolce & Gabbana, Gucci, Versace) as well as frock stars Etro and Issa. Cavern Walks centre (www.cavern-walks.com) is another hotspot of trend-alert boutiques – a bulging bag from Cricket is a badge of honour among label lovers. Liverpool One is the £9 billion shopping centre that opened in 2008 (www.liverpool-one.com).

Something for nothing Pier Head, in the heart of Liverpool Docks, gives you the best view of the Three Graces: the Royal Liver Building, the Cunard Building and the Port of Liverpool Building. These 19th-century edifices are monuments to the city's historic commercial prowess.

Don't go home without... a bag of black and white Everton mints, so-called because a woman known as 'the Toffee Lady' used to sell the stripy sweets before kick-off at Everton's home football matches.

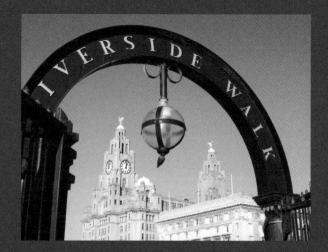

LITERALLY LIVERPOOL

Beatlemania is still going strong here. The Beatles Story in Albert Dock tells the tale of John, Paul, George and Ringo, complete with walk-through yellow submarine (www.beatlesstory. com). Fab Four fans can tour the childhood homes of Lennon and McCartney – now owned by the National Trust and restored to their original 1950s glory (www.nationaltrust.org.uk/beatles).

DIARY

February Chinese New Year is enthusiastically celebrated in the city's Chinatown. **March** LEAP, a diverse festival of contemporary dance showcasing the talents of the Liverpool Institute for Performing Arts (www.merseysidedance.co.uk). **April** The Grand National meeting at nearby Aintree Racecourse (www.aintree.co.uk). Liverpool Boat Show in historic Albert Dock and surroundings goes on until the first week of May (www.liverpoolboatshow.com). **August** The massive Mathew Street Music Festival brings several stages to a number of city locations and features performances by emerging and established local groups (www.mathewstreetfestival. com). International Beatles Week attracts more than 200 bands from around the world to play tribute to the city's favourite sons, with markets and exhibitions dedicated to the famous foursome (www.cavernclub.org/beatle_week.php). The flagship Creamfields festival sees international DJs and live acts bid the summer farewell (www.creamfieldsfestival.co.uk).

Hope Street Hotel

STYLE Open-plan elegance
SETTING Lofty Liverpool palazzo

'The huge wooden tub, with fluffy towels and Ren products, is big enough for two with a plush armchair opposite, so you can quibble over who soaks and who watches'

When pondering new mini-break options, I've never previously found myself saying, 'Ooh, Liverpool'. But that was before we discovered the chic boutique treat of staying at the Hope Street Hotel. When we find out that it's just a quick walk from Lime Street Station, it seems daft to do anything but travel from London by train. The journey from Euston is surprisingly swift, marred only slightly by a post-10-pints passenger who joins at the penultimate stop.

At the station, milliseconds pass before a guy drops everything to give us directions. 'Go up this road until you see a bombed-out church,' he begins, before mapping out the 15-minute route. Picturing bleak ruins, we wonder if our destination is quite right for Mr & Mrs Smith-style romance. But, when we get to our HQ for the weekend, we apologise to Merseyside and all who sail in her. Billed as Liverpool's 'first boutique hotel', the Hope Street Hotel is within the city's cultural quarter, where you'll find many restaurants and theatres, as well as the art deco Philharmonic Hall. The hotel building dates from 1860, but it is all modern minimalism inside, with a softly lit reception and low sofas in the lounge.

Mercifully, the receptionist who shows us to our suite forgoes the typical fastidious room tour ('That's the phone – really? And that's the door?'), leaving the fun exploration stuff to us. Mr Smith starts playing with the Bang & Olufsen TV and sound system. I manage to hold back from jumping on the Egyptian-cotton-sheeted bed, but admire the room's USPs: huge wooden beams, touch-on light switches, open-plan X-factor bathroom on an upper level. 'I want that bath,' I announce. 'Where can I get that bath?' I'm transfixed by the huge, freestanding wooden tub, accessorised with fluffy towels and Ren products. The thing is clearly big enough for two, but there's a plush leather armchair opposite, so you can quibble over who soaks and who gets to watch. For soakaphobes, there's a huge glass-fronted shower, and double basins, complete with mist-free mirrors.

We dine in the hotel's renowned restaurant, the London Carriage Works. The atmosphere is nicely busy and buzzy, the wine list never-ending, and the food incredible: all delicious, fresh, local and organic produce. It doesn't hurt that chef Paul Askew's cosmopolitan flavours are served in a grand property built at the end of the 19th century in the style of a Venetian palazzo. A private party means the hotel bar is off-limits, but it isn't exactly a hardship sloping off to our suite to enjoy a couple of brandies there.

The bed – big enough to lose yourself in for a week – is tough to leave the next morning, particularly when the smoked salmon and scrambled egg breakfast arrives. But we finally haul ourselves up and out for an explore. Shopping-wise, Liverpool's city centre has all the usual high-street favourites and so on, as well as independent and designer boutiques: Cricket at the Cavern centre, and Flannels at the Met Quarter. You may not be a celeb-mag reader, but you have to have been in media exile not to have seen them swinging in bag-form at some point from a Wag's arms in the ubiquitous paparazzi shots. And the atmosphere in town is chirpy – 10 times friendlier than what we're used to down in the capital. 'That looks lovely,' says one woman, as I step out of a changing-room cubicle – and she is another shopper, not the retail assistant selling me Vivienne Westwood I can't afford.

Tate Liverpool in the Albert Dock is a new Tate for us, and well worth our time. Sadly our visit wasn't timed to catch the Turner Prize exhibition, held here as a curtain-raiser for Liverpool's status as European Capital of Culture 2008. The area

'We're seduced by its big squishy sofas and delicious champagne cocktails'

in general is an agreeable place to wander around; we even get to enjoy our first outdoor drink of the year. Then it's back home – aka Bang & Olufsen plus bed, for an afternoon movie and a snooze – perfect.

Evening meanders its way down the Mersey and we're pleased to learn that Hope Street is packed with restaurants, including the recommended 60 Hope Street and the Side Door – but, we stumble across Valparaiso, just around the corner on Hardman Street. Liverpool's only Chilean restaurant, it does a mean steak, and their traditional corn and mince pie is delicious, too.

After dinner we check out the hotel bar, where a pianist bashes out requests – Coldplay, not show tunes – on her Steinway Grand. We're seduced by its big squishy sofas and delicious champagne cocktails; the atmosphere is energised yet relaxed, with a clientele that we guess is a mixture of locals and Hope Street guests.

You can have breakfast in the hotel restaurant, but we're now utterly addicted to our suite, which I have, by this point, decided I'll be replicating as the ultimate one-bed back home. We summon a trayful of toasted bagels in bed. 'Room 406? Is that... Ms X?' I'm asked, on calling room service. No, I tell them. 'I know that name,' I say to Mr Smith. 'Isn't she a fashion designer?' He looks puzzled, then it clicks. We're sharing the Hope Street Hotel with a much-photographed British pop minx. I have to admit, I quite like being mistaken for a pop star. And looking around the suite, I feel a bit like one, too.

Reviewed by Claire Baylis

NEED TO KNOW

Rooms 89, including seven suites and two penthouses.
Rates £89–£650. Continental breakfast, £12.50; full English, £15.50. A la carte breakfast menu also available.
Check-out Weekdays, 11am; weekends, midday. Later check-outs charged at £10 an hour, subject to availability.
Facilities Free WiFi, DVD/CD library. In rooms, wall-mounted LCD TV, DVD/CD player, free broadband internet access, underfloor heating, mist-free mirrors, rain shower heads, Ren toiletries, minifridge/champagne chiller in some rooms.
Children Games available; kitchen accommodating. Cots and extra beds for under-14s can be provided in the studio rooms, at no extra cost. There are also DVDs and CDs for children.
Also In-room beauty treatments can be arranged, and small pets can be put up – a cleaning fee of £30 will be charged.

IN THE KNOW

Our favourite rooms Suite 406 is an open-plan suite with a sloping ceiling, exposed beams and a mezzanine bathroom with a huge Italian wooden bathtub. All suites have oak flooring and Bang & Olufsen TVs and DVD players.
Hotel bar The Residents' Lounge is a cocktail bar (open Thursdays to Saturdays only) with table service and live music – watch out for ivory tinklers on the Steinway grand piano and try one of the Pimm's Royale champagne cocktails. The restaurant bar is open seven days a week.
Hotel restaurant Paul Askew – a fan of the 'three ways' method – is chef at the London Carriage Works restaurant, which offers a choice of menus, including à la carte, pre-theatre and tasting menus. His grown-up Modern International culinary bent is evident in dishes such as confit shoulder of black-faced Suffolk lamb and pan-roasted sea-bass.
Top table Table 15, nestled between the restaurant's decorative glass shards.
Room service 24 hours: an all-day menu including market specials, with a limited night menu available 10pm–7am.
Dress code Relaxed and urbane.
Local knowledge Visit the Everyman Liverpool and/or Liverpool Playhouse theatres, both of which are leading a resurgence of fine drama in the city (www.everymanplayhouse.com); the hotel can check ticket availability for you.

LOCAL EATING AND DRINKING

A smart, great-value basement bistro beneath the theatre of the same name, Everyman Bistro (0151 708 9545) has a daily changing menu of Francophile tarts, flans and quiches. 60 Hope Street (0151 707 6060) has an impressive fine-dining room upstairs, a bar, and a cosier café on the ground floor. While Caribbean-themed Alma De Cuba on Seel Street (0151 702 7394) attracts the footballers' wives and popstrels of Liverpool, it is also a great cocktail bar in a beautiful 18th-century church building. Clove Hitch on Hope Street (0151 709 6574) serves classic Brit dishes such as bangers and mash, as well as more exotic offerings such as swordfish with chimichurri and orange-glazed carrots. Leave room for a home-made pudding. Opposite the hotel, Host (0151 708 5831) is a first-class option for pan-Asian dining. The Shipping Forecast on Slater Street (0151 709 6901) hails itself an alehouse and eatery and the spot to head for live music and great beers.

GET A ROOM!

For more information, or to book this hotel, go to www.mrandmrssmith.com. Register your Smith membership card (see pages 4–5) to enjoy exclusive offers and privileges.

 SMITH MEMBER OFFER A bottle of prosecco on arrival, plus free late check-out (usually charged at £10 an hour and subject to availability).

Hope Street Hotel 40 Hope Street, Liverpool L1 9DA (0151 709 3000; www.hopestreethotel.co.uk)

LONDON

CITYSCAPE Multidimensional mega-sprawl
CITY LIFE Cosmopolitan, cultured, eccentric

London is effortlessly cool – and unashamed of flaunting it. From the revived East End to the swish haunts of Notting Hill, it accessorises its heritage beauty with couldn't-give-a-damn street cred. This feisty lady has it all: glorious parks and historic squares, monuments galore, museums piled with colonial swag, galleries where art soothes or surprises, and stages attracting theatre's hottest talent. A multi-ethnic English eccentric, the British capital lets you eat and shop your way around the globe, sending you home sated and satisfied. The Routemaster buses, King's Road punks and Carnaby Street swingers may be long gone, but this shoppers' Valhalla has reinvented itself as a modern metropolis. And, while architectural icons the Gherkin, the London Eye and Wembley Stadium provide a skyline for the new renaissance, the build-up to the 2012 Olympics provides an endlessly fascinating topic for the city's enthusiastic cabbies...

GETTING THERE

Planes London has several international airports: Heathrow, to the west, is on the Piccadilly Line, or 15 minutes from Paddington on the Heathrow Express (www.heathrowexpress.com). Gatwick, to the south, is 30 minutes from Victoria via the Gatwick Express (www. gatwickexpress.com). Stansted and Luton, to the north, are where most of the budget carriers land.
Trains International trains arrive at St Pancras (www. stpancras.com), which has good links via the Underground. The Tube will be your saviour (www.tfl.gov.uk/tube).
Automobiles On weekdays from 7am to 6pm, there's a £10 daily Congestion Charge payable to drive into central London (www.cclondon.com); parking can be costly.
Boats There are commuter and leisure boats all along the river: see www.tfl.gov.uk/river for timetables and routes.

LOCAL KNOWLEDGE

Taxis You can hail one of London's trademark hackney cabs anywhere, or ring Zingo (0870 070 0700) from your mobile, and the nearest one will find you. Avoid unlicensed minicabs; we recommend Climatecars (020 7350 5960), whose carbon-neutral minicabs operate in central London

Packing tips A pocket-sized *A–Z* guide with a Tube map will prevent 'Where am I?' moments becoming 'Lost' moments.
Recommended reads Martin Amis' *London Fields* follows three characters as nuclear disaster looms; Iain Sinclair circumnavigated the M25 on foot to research *London Orbital*; Peter Ackroyd's epic *London: The Biography* treats the town as a personality.
Local specialities London wins global praise for its authentic multi-cultural cuisine, from Chinatown's dim sum to Brick Lane's saucy spices and West London's Moroccan tagines... But, hey, even a mega-metropolis can source from its own garden. At Oliver Rowe's King's Cross restaurant, Konstam at the Prince Albert (020 7833 5040), all the ingredients used in the making of his Northern European menu are grown or produced within the M25. Norbury Blue cheese, Tower Hill honey and Amersham lamb not only lack air miles, they also offer a true taste of London town.
Perfect picnic The 791-acre expanse of Hampstead Heath has panoramic views, secret woods and enough grass to spread a rug out and still have room to get a good Frisbee session going. Fill up your hamper at the nearby Rosslyn Delicatessen (020 7794 9210).

And... London moves so quickly that, by the time you've heard about that hot club, exhibition or under-the-radar boutique, chances are it's, like, so over. Tag along with an Urban Gentry guide, however, and you'll get an up-to-the-minute take on city life; choose from themed tours including Art Insider, East End Hip and Market Fresh, or get them to tailor a bespoke itinerary around your tastes. See www.urbangentry.com for details.

WORTH GETTING OUT OF BED FOR

Viewpoint Book a ride on the London Eye, the South Bank's big wheel (www.londoneye.com), for sight-spotting and vertigo-inducing views of five counties. Then amble over Waterloo Bridge at sunset to reacquaint yourself with the cityscape from the ground. Want to work harder for your views? Climb the spiral steps of St Paul's Cathedral to the Whispering Gallery and then up and out to the Stone and Golden Galleries for magnificent panoramic views of the capital. At King Henry's Mound in Richmond Park, six miles away, there are incredible westward vistas of Berkshire – plus an amazing view back to St Paul's.

Arts and culture London has a wealth of cultural delights to tickle all tastes: Tate Modern and Tate Britain house British and international art collections (www.tate.org.uk). Hoxton's White Cube gallery (www.whitecube.com) is edgier, or, for the experimental and out there, pop in on the art studios and galleries lining Vyner Street in Bethnal Green. Arm yourself with a copy of weekly listings magazine *Time Out* for the latest information about what's on; and visit www.ticketmaster.co.uk to book seats at anything from West End musicals or plays at the Globe Theatre to stand-up comedy and pop concerts.

Activities Cool off at the Serpentine Lido, where you can sling yourself into a deckchair, paddle, or show off your 110-yard crawl (www.serpentinelido.com). Or see the city on blades: roll up for the Urban Rites Friday Night Skate (www.thefns.com) and just follow the pack through the city streets. No skates? That's no excuse: hire some from Slick Willies on Gloucester Road (020 7225 0004) and you can wheel wherever the wind blows you.

Daytripper Catch the boat from Embankment Pier to maritime-tastic Greenwich. Check out the covered arts and crafts market, the National Maritime Museum (www.nmm.ac.uk) and the Royal Observatory (www.rog.nmm.ac.uk), where you can, literally, straddle time, before chilling over a pint of real ale in a historic pub, such as the Trafalgar Tavern (020 8858 2909).

Children The Natural History Museum (www.nhm.ac.uk) in South Kensington keeps those obsessed with dinosaurs or body parts enthralled. In winter, ice-skating rinks freeze into life all over town. The one at Somerset House was the first, and is still the best (www.somerset-house.org.uk).

Walks For city strolling, head for the river, then stick with it. Try the towpath from Richmond, Putney or Chiswick for leafy ambling. In town, take in the South Bank from Westminster to Tower Bridge, ticking the reconstructed *Golden Hinde* galleon (www.goldenhinde.com) and City Hall (aka the Leaning Tower of Pizzas) off your to-see list.

Shopping Knightsbridge and Bond Street are the designer-label doyennes, but for something you can't get at home, a market's the place: Camden is good for vintage threads and clubwear; over east, Spitalfields is best for funky fashion finds; early birds get the best blooms at Columbia Road Flower Market; for organic food-tasting opportunities try Borough Market; Portobello Road is a must-go for antiques and vintage fashion.

Something for nothing Entrance to many of London's museums is still free (www.londonnet.co.uk/museums). In summer, pull up a pew on the South Bank: before long, street theatre will start happening all around you.

Don't go home without... taking traditional high tea. Go high luxe at Claridge's (020 7409 6307); high art at the Wallace Collection restaurant (020 7563 9500); or high fashion at the Berkeley (020 7235 6000) – its 'Prêt-à-portea' cakes are modelled on must-have Anya Hindmarch and Marc Jacobs designs, and modishly served on Paul Smith china.

LAUDABLY LONDON

At Hyde Park's Speakers' Corner (www.speakerscorner.net) you are guaranteed the right to free speech. Drag your soapbox along on a Sunday afternoon and get whatever's perplexing you off your chest. You'll be in good company: Karl Marx, William Morris and George Orwell have all spouted their views here over the decades. Be prepared for vigorous heckling, though.

DIARY

March Oxford and Cambridge Boat Race from Putney to Mortlake (www.theboatrace.org). April The London Marathon: a 26-mile race for athletes, fundraisers and mentalists in diving suits (www.virginlondonmarathon.co.uk). May Chelsea Flower Show brings marvellous blooms to SW3 (www.rhs.org.uk/chelsea). June The Wimbledon Championships send the capital tennis mad for a fortnight (www.wimbledon.org). July–September The BBC Proms concerts (www.bbc.co.uk/proms). August Notting Hill Carnival, a float-filled, bass-thumping weekend of musical mayhem. September Open House Weekend sees 600 buildings, old and new, let the public in free (www.londonopenhouse.org). October London Film Festival (www. lff.org.uk). November On Guy Fawkes' Night, there are fireworks displays in parks all over town; book an eighth-floor table at the Oxo Tower (020 7803 3888) for a premium view of the Lord Mayor's fireworks on the river. London Jazz Festival – nice (www.serious.org.uk).

Bingham

STYLE Trendy townhouse
SETTING Richmond riverside

'Winding our way through leafy lanes,
we feel as though we're visiting a country
village without even having to leave
London, and we like it'

When my other half suggests an exciting weekend jaunt, my inner spoiled brat jumps up and down, thinking: 'Yay... Will it be a boutique hotel in the Cotswolds – or maybe somewhere super-glam like Cannes?' When we jump in the car and the SatNav announces 'seven miles to your destination', my hopes aren't at their highest. Then Mr Smith mentions that he has another fantastic surprise. His eyes wander down to an envelope at my feet. Oh no. I'm sure I can make out 'Twickenham Stadium' through the address window. A rugby match in southwest London isn't exactly my dream date. Fantasies involving oversized Gucci shades on La Croisette and cream teas in the genteel hills evaporate, replaced by chanting, beer-swilling sports fans...

Richmond has never been my top choice for a weekend escape but, winding our way through leafy lanes, we feel as though we're visiting a country village without even having to leave London, and we like it. As we pull up at the Bingham, I'm back on track towards those hopes of boutique hotel-based shenanigans. We're definitely somewhere stylish. Inside, the roll-call of chic is answered in full: droplet chandeliers, Osborne & Little wallpaper, mushroom-hued Farrow & Ball, burnt-red leather tub chairs. (I ask Mr Smith to suggest a description for the colour, and he volunteers 'Superman's pants'. I contest that that would make them pillar-box red, which they are not. He replies, in the same tone an artist might use to someone who admits they can't tell a Braque from a Picasso: 'Not in the recent version. I think you'll find they're a darker tone.' Oh, what would I do without his erudite cultural references?)

We're led up to an attic room on the second floor, which is a little light on vistas, owing to the angle of the windows, so staff kindly redirect us to the best room, named after the poetess Sappho. With an unadulterated river view over the lawn, through huge floor-to-ceiling French windows, it is along far more romantic lines. Weeping willows, rowers on the water – who needs the South of France after all?

We head out for a stroll. A small festival is underway on the grassy knoll in front of a full deck of wine-bar chain outposts, always packed in the summer months. A live band is playing, and lots of happy souls are whiling away

the afternoon, drinks in hands, swaying to music. After stocking up on bathtime treats from the L'Occitane on the high street (there's a Jacuzzi big enough for two back in our bathroom), we treat ourselves to souvenirs from a delightful chocolatier, William Curley, hidden on a lane off the main drag. It's definitely starting to feel like a holiday. We retreat to Bingham for a cup of tea on the lawn. In a few seconds, the world of pushchairs and M&S bags has given way to something a lot more *Swallows and Amazons*.

After a pre-dinner freshen-up (if a long soak in the tub with the crossword merits the description), voices outside suggest that a private party is getting underway here at the hotel. Mr Smith takes a look out of the window to investigate, forgetting he's fresh from the bath, much to the horror/delight of a group of girls walking past by the river. I investigate the party and recognise some faces

– what fun! (Thank goodness it hadn't been them admiring the black wrought-iron balconies on this fine Georgian property minutes earlier.) Holidaying in your hometown is even better when dinner is followed by a shindig with friends. After our delicious meal at riverside restaurant Gaucho and, more noticeably, a bottle of Weinert Malbec, the dancefloor back at Bingham is unavoidable. Following a bit of Saturday Night Feverishness, Mr Smith decides a more civilised end to our evening might lie in a nightcap and a game of chess in the hotel's upstairs lounge. But about two moves in, it's clear I'm as much a threat to Kasparov as Mr Smith is to John Travolta – and the only king I care about is the bed awaiting us in our river-view room.

After a prize-winningly peaceful night's sleep – it really is like being in the countryside – I take a look out the window to see it's the kind of overcast day you're always secretly

grateful for, because it's an excuse to stay holed up in your big bed with fluffy cushions and widescreen TV. When I phone reception and ask for eggs Florentine and toast for breakfast, my needs are greeted with warmth. Pretty soon, a couple of baskets of bread and pastries sufficient to feed a rugby team is with us. Which reminds me... What about those tickets I'd spotted?

Fast forward a few hours and we've dozed off, only to be woken by housekeeping at the door. Oops. We're still in bed. The good ol' English embarrassment gene kicks in. 'I hope they don't think that we're up to mischief,' I say, blushing. Mr Smith sighs. 'We're in a hotel – it's not that they suspect it; they expect it.' We emerge at lunchtime, and I affect the demeanour of someone who's well-rested but, at the same time, doesn't have too much of a spring in her step.

We've decided on a Richmond Sunday roast in the restaurant, where we discover that we're not just getting fed, but that there's also a guitar-strumming Jose Feliciano-alike chanteur to treat us to some live music. Should I ask if he'll play some Rolling Stones, suggests Mr Smith? Then the penny drops – that's what the tickets are for! There was I, wishing for an out-of-town escapade, when he'd got a fantastic adventure planned in London. You can't always get what you want – but in this case, what I got turned out to be better than what I thought I wanted.

Reviewed by Juliet Kinsman

NEED TO KNOW

Rooms 15.

Rates £190–£285. Continental breakfast, £12; full English, £15.

Check-out 11am, but a later check-out is sometimes possible. Earliest check-in, 3pm (can be earlier, subject to availability).

Facilities Gardens, free WiFi throughout. In rooms, flatscreen TV, DVD/CD library, iPod dock and sound system, minibar.

Children Under-12s stay free, with no cost for extra beds. Over-12s, £50 a night. Babysitting can be arranged. The hotel is well-equipped with baby monitors, cots, highchairs and a nappy-changing room, and Superior River Double room Sappho can be connected to a smaller double for families.

Also Massages or beauty treatments and use of a local gym can be arranged on request. No pets, but guide dogs are welcome. On-site parking is limited, but spaces in the carpark opposite are pre-bookable at a cost of £10 a day.

IN THE KNOW

Our favourite rooms Extremely spacious and with an incredible Thames view, Sappho is the best choice. Callirrhoe has an antique four-poster bed. Baudelaire also has a sumptuous four-poster, plus a walk-in shower and whirlpool bath for two. Borgia has a leafy vista. If a river view is vital to you, specify this when booking.

Hotel bar The lounge bar is a relaxed, retro-style, leather-armchairs kinda venue overlooking the river.

Hotel restaurant Shay Cooper's Michelin-starred food is Modern British, with traditional roasts on Sundays. The airy dining room on the ground floor is all chic neutrals and art deco mirrors inside, with a decked terrace outside that looks out over the gardens and riverside. The restaurant is closed on Sunday evenings.

Top table By the window, with a river view; romantics will want a table on the covered balcony.

Room service Lunch and dinner can be served in your room, as can sandwiches, plates of charcuterie or cheese, smoked salmon and, within reason, whatever you like.

Dress code City-to-country chic.

Local knowledge Hop on a river ferry at St Helena Pier, just by Richmond Bridge, and float gently down the Thames all the way to historic Hampton Court Palace (www.hrp.org.uk); ring Turks Launches on 020 8546 2434 to check times.

LOCAL EATING AND DRINKING

Lovers of French food will enjoy **Chez Lindsay** (020 8948 7473), a bistro on Richmond's Hill Rise where Lindsay Wotton's Breton cuisine takes centre stage: try griddled galettes or cider-soaked oysters. Along the towpath, with an alfresco terrace, modern Argentine restaurant and bar **Gaucho** (020 8948 4030) is a carnivore's dream come true: the big draw is steak, in all its seared, grilled and well-hung glory (although there are vegetarian and seafood dishes). The acclaimed **Petersham Nurseries Café** is a 10-minute stroll across Petersham Meadows. Book well in advance to sample Skye Gyngell's garden-fresh seasonal menus (020 8940 5230). Downriver in Kew, **The Glasshouse** on Station Parade (020 8940 6777) is an acclaimed eatery for a special-occasion lunch or romantic dinner; Anthony Boyd oversees the fancy French-influenced flavours in this elegant cream-coloured restaurant. Ask for a window table. Family-run restaurant **Enoteca Turi** on Putney High Street (020 8785 4449) has an awe-inspiring 350-bin wine list, with superb regional Italian dishes to match.

GET A ROOM!

For more information, or to book this hotel, go to www.mrandmrssmith.com. Register your Smith membership card (see pages 4–5) to enjoy exclusive offers and privileges.

SMITH MEMBER OFFER A chilled half-bottle of champagne, plus free late check-out (subject to availability).

Bingham 61–63 Petersham Road, Richmond, Surrey TW10 6UT (020 8940 0902; www.thebingham.co.uk)

Haymarket Hotel

STYLE Witty British bolthole
SETTING Theatreland thoroughfare

'The swimming pool's Yves Klein-blue
18-metre splendour sparkles
under twinkling lights, flanked by
a fully stocked bar'

A brisk five-minute walk from my office on Savile Row, through the crowds of meandering tourists gawping at the bright lights of London's West End, and I'm already in the lobby of my stylish stay for the night, bang on Haymarket. This feels strange; I only live 10 minutes down the road. 'Have you come far?' enquires the smiling person at the front desk, glancing at my miniscule piece of luggage. Before I can elaborate with some convoluted story involving lost bags or builders, Mrs Smith arrives, carrying even less. Would we be using the same name throughout our stay? A 'yes' from me, and a 'no' from Mrs Smith induces a knowing grin from the receptionist, who obviously thinks we've only just met in an internet chatroom, and have decided right away that the most upmarket place to initiate an illicit affair is at this hip hotel round the corner from Trafalgar Square.

A cursory tour of the ground-floor guest areas takes us through an airy, art-filled conservatory, a sultry, sofa-filled library and an elegant drawing room, giving us a chance to take in Kit Kemp's signature classic-yet-quirky clash of fabrics and furnishings, before being escorted up to our suite. At this point I remember having heard the word 'upgrade' mentioned – and when I see the size of our quarters, I realise this actually does mean that we're about to experience the hotel equivalent of turning left as you board the front of a 747. The simple fact that our new abode has four doorways indicates to us that it's first class; add to that two bathrooms, a bedroom and a living room.

After a quick scoot around, deciding who's having which bathroom, we collapse on a plump sofa to take in our breezy modern British surroundings. The view from our bed is of a timeless, distinguished London side street, a beautiful Nash building mirroring our own fine Regency dwelling. This is a place where country-house charm meets London sophistication, where the home-from-home atmosphere is a refreshing departure from the usual five-star offerings in this postcode. We concur it would be the perfect base for a Hollywood star staying for an extended period while treading the boards locally; a hunch that is later evidenced when we just catch a famous face dart behind the Tony Cragg sculpture in reception. The 50-room Haymarket prides itself on all of its sleeping

salons having a unique personality. This is no temple to minimalism: fresh colours and textures abound, not to mention old and antique furniture of various shapes and sizes. The super-high bed reminds me of the kind usually only experienced from behind a velvet rope, when you're dragged around stately homes as a child. Among Mrs Smith's professional accomplishments are fabric and textile design, and eyeing up the pretty, contemporary chintz of the curtains, with candy-striped cushions and boldly upholstered padded headboards, she declares it wonderfully cosy and comfortable. A compliment not to be sniffed at when delivered by a native of Sweden, where tastes lean towards a simpler, more functional approach to decor.

Sure, there are museums, theatres, shops and nightlife galore here in St James's. But, by now officially in holiday mode (despite it being a workday on home soil), Mrs Smith and I forgo plans to see a film at the Institute of Contemporary Arts in favour of the novelty of slipping into swimwear for a pre-dinner dip. The pool is in the basement, and my initial fear of a glorified birdbath in a strip-lighting-illuminated dungeon couldn't have been more misplaced. Its Yves Klein-blue 18-metre splendour sparkles under twinkling lights, flanked by a fully stocked bar along one wall and a sprinkling of gold chaises longues. This is a fantasy grotto for grown-ups and, amplifying the 'Club Tropicana' kitsch appeal, on our visit, half of it is covered up with a temporary dancefloor. Sadly, before we've a chance to wonder if the 'drinks are free', and just as we're poised to plunge into the inviting water, someone pops their head round the door to apologetically announce that it's reserved for a one-off event – a rarity, we're told. Still, the needle on our imaginary Wham! soundtrack comes to a screeching halt, and we trudge back to our boudoir, plotting to return later. As a decent alternative to splashing about in public, we decide that the marble bathrooms might

compensate for our swimmus interruptus. Filling the bath, and pouring in a cocktail of the Miller Harris potions, we luxuriate in a haze of sweet scents for an episode of *The Simpsons* on the big flatscreen TV. Not quite as highbrow as the ICA documentary but, as the remote bobs in the water like a new-age rubber duck, we agree it's probably a damn sight more fun.

As an aficionado of the Piccadilly locale, I'm familiar with what this well-trodden patch of central London has on offer. So, heading for the hotel's own eatery, Brumus, suits us just fine. With its own potent colours and cunningly contrasting textures (but of a darker and richer variety), the restaurant has an intimate and, dare I say it, romantic feel. We're shown to our seats by the window, and having briefly looked at the menus, we reach across the table to hold hands and simultaneously gaze out onto this famous London street – and note the less-than-starry-eyed souls queuing for the 159 bus outside.

As darkness falls, we become more invisible to the throngs outside and are soon entertained by the comings and goings of excited *Phantom of the Opera* ticket-holders across the road. The people-watching reveals more eccentricities than the international cuisine, which plays it a little safer than you'd expect in such a bold habitat. Still, that doesn't stop us enjoying one too many glasses of something chilled and Italian in blissed-out comfort, and down the corridor we bounce towards our suite. We're a little thrown by voices emanating from our room; a quick double-check – it's definitely the right number. Ahh, the bedside radio has been tuned into something classical. 'How cosy,' proclaims Mrs Smith again. Although this time there's a glint in her eye. I'm hoping that means the last thing on her mind is an appreciation of the upholstery...

Reviewed by Sean Dixon

NEED TO KNOW

Rooms 50, including 17 suites, and a separate two- to five-bedroom townhouse.

Rates Doubles, £312–£408; Junior Suites, £492–£565; Superior Suites, from £2,100 up to £5,400 for a two- to five-bedroom townhouse. Rates exclude breakfast (£19.50 a person).

Check-out 11am, although this is flexible. Earliest check-in, 2pm.

Facilities Heated indoor pool, gym, treatment room, library, valet parking. In rooms, minibar, flatscreen TV and DVD player, CD player and iPod dock, WiFi (£20 for 24 hours), Miller Harris toiletries.

Children Cots and beds are free for under-12s; over-12s are £40. Babysitting can be booked. Games on request.

Also Smoking rooms are available.

IN THE KNOW

Our favourite rooms Each room has its own palette of hues and patterns; we loved blue and brown Room 2, although it's on the ground floor, which isn't the quietest. Large corner rooms 111, 211 and 311 on the floors above have the same colour scheme. Deluxe doubles facing the courtyard are romantic. For wonderful views of London's rooftops, get one of the smaller top-floor rooms; 402 has low-slung windows, giving it a first-class Haymarket vista. Junior Suite 100 has outdoor decking.

Hotel bar During the day, the bar provides a place to pause for a cappuccino, or after the sun is past the yard-arm, a few Haymarket Cosmos or Brumus Margaritas. Doors close at 11.45, but those in situ can carry on regardless till 1am.

Hotel restaurant Brightly coloured Brumus Bar & Restaurant provides European brasserie classics, care of Taofiq Adegoroye's excellent kitchen brigade. Open 7am–11pm (11.45pm for the post-theatre menu and bar snacks).

Top table We loved the cosy tables in the bar area; at night, a window seat is fun, but in daylight you might feel on view.

Room service Available 24 hours a day.

Dress code Savile Row sharpness or low-key London luxe.

Local knowledge You're surrounded by London's leading stages here, including the Theatre Royal Haymarket (www.trh.co.uk). If you haven't booked ahead (www.officiallondontheatre.co.uk), visit the 'tkts' booth in Leicester Square, where boards list cut-price last-minute tickets for that day's matinee and evening performances.

LOCAL EATING AND DRINKING

For a traditional British experience, with a sprinkling of pomp, head to The Wolseley on Piccadilly (020 7499 6996) for lunch or tea, or to Bentley's Oyster Bar & Grill on Swallow Street (020 7734 4756): slurp oysters at the marble-topped champagne bar while pianists tickle the ivories; or dine upstairs, where Richard Corrigan works his magic in the Grill restaurant. Hakkasan on Hanway Place (020 7927 7000) has to be the sexiest Chinese restaurant ever; and it was the first to earn a Michelin star. Just off Regent Street, Veeraswamy (020 7734 1401) is the capital's oldest Indian eatery, but it couldn't feel more contemporary after its makeover. At The Ivy on West Street (020 7836 4751), you can brush shoulders with gossiping showbiz legends over classic British dishes. If you're in the mood to splurge, multi-venue Sketch on Conduit Street (020 7659 4500) offers flashy French-fusion fantasies, brasserie fare, cocktails, or delicate patisseries in its tearoom.

GET A ROOM!

For more information, or to book this hotel, go to www.mrandmrssmith.com. Register your Smith membership card (see pages 4–5) to enjoy exclusive offers and privileges.

 SMITH MEMBER OFFER A bottle of house champagne.

Haymarket Hotel 1 Suffolk Place, London SW1Y 4HX (020 7470 4000; www.haymarkethotel.com)

High Road House

STYLE Cool members' club outpost
SETTING Boulevard in the 'burbs

'I could quite happily have planted myself in the freestanding tub by the bed, with Mr Smith, the two bottles of champagne and the chocolate'

‘Ah, you've got a very special room,' said the man on reception mysteriously, as Mr Smith and I checked into High Road House, the Chiswick outpost of Nick Jones' Soho House empire. 'Very special' was reiterated by an elfin-type creature dressed head-to-toe in black, who had appeared at our sides, smiling and rubbing his hands with glee. Very special is good, I thought, but I wouldn't expect anything else from the savvy Mr Jones, and his oft-enlisted interiors whiz, Ilse Crawford. He's been serving up a cocktail of high style, designer comfort and brasserie food to the media masses in his 'houses' for the better part of two decades.

Why our particular room was worthy of fanfare was finally revealed when we made our way to the third floor, took a right down the stripy-purple-carpeted corridor and turned the key of room number nine. It's a vast, gleaming white space, in which the only splashes of colour are afforded by a yellow wooden chair hanging on a hook and a green cashmere blanket on the bed. We smiled.

After the flash of snow-blindness had cleared, the nuances of the room became apparent. There is a freestanding bedside bath big enough for two (or even three media luvvies, should they so desire) poised at one end, a retro Bush radio discreetly wafting Radio 3 over the airwaves, a large flatscreen TV on a swivel to ensure comfortable aquatic viewing, a king-size bed, piled high with nimbus-like pillows, and two white leather and chrome armchairs. As usual, I scurried to open all the drawers, which are helpfully labelled: 'teatime' is stocked with charming miniature Le Parfait jars of hot chocolate; 'builders' has teabags, coffee and sugar; 'tuck box' is a sweet tooth's paradise; and 'cold' is the minibar, offering wine, champagne, fresh milk, Coke, beer and bars of Melt organic chocolate. I could quite happily have planted myself in the bath, with Mr Smith, the two bottles of champagne and the chocolate. There, we'd flick through the endless Sky channels in a leisurely fashion, only to decamp to the bed hours later, in shrively-toed, bathrobed bliss, for room-service comfort food. But it was only 4pm, and such sybaritic behaviour would have to wait.

It's not surprising that Jones chose Chiswick for one of his ventures. No longer is this West London location the preserve of the posh middle-to-ageing population. It's still well-heeled of course, but the lush leafy suburb with its attractive houses is also home to younger power couples, with babies in Bill Amberg papooses, wanting their children to have access to good schools and green spaces, musicians, artists, journalists and writers – all of whom are the perfect target audience for the Soho House brand.

Heading outdoors, you're on Chiswick High Road, which is a notch above most of the city's high street offerings. The Gourmet Burger Bar is W4's answer to the golden arches; there are lots of independent shops; and Turnham Green Terrace, just around the corner, is a foodie's delight – its greengrocer, fishmonger, baker, butcher, chocolatier and deli remind us of the streets of yesteryear, with not a Tesco in sight (that's back on the High Road). The real find, though, was just next-door: the Old Cinema is an antiques emporium, set out over three floors and full of everything from old postcards and French glassware to vintage fashion and leather armchairs. I clocked up a mental bill of thousands of pounds on our whistle-stop window-shopping tour. Flanking the other side of the hotel's busy brasserie is the Cowshed

Turnham Green Terrace is a foodie's delight; its baker, butcher, chocolatier and deli remind us of yesteryear'

shop, selling the raft of Soho House's on-trend own-brand spa products, a selection of which resides by the bath upstairs. With names such as Saucy Cow, Wild Cow and Cheeky Cow, I couldn't wait to add something naughty to the waters, putting paid to the mooted idea of an afternoon's shopping in Richmond. In fact, even a visit to glorious Kew Gardens, just down the river and at our ambling disposal, was gazumped by the draw of a larger-than-life, full-body dunking.

Back upstairs, I had to lure Mr Smith into my enormous bubbly bedroom tub, as he seemed more interested in the lily pad-sized shower head in the bathroom. But, in the end, he couldn't resist the chance to watch *The Pink Panther* while wet, so we slopped around and slathered ourselves with the bovine unguents until we noticed it was martini hour.

We debated whether or not to sip our cocktails over a game of pool in the louche-looking, low-lit 'Playroom', but settled instead for the more glamorous surrounds of the members' bar, which better suited my freshly piquant chilli and passion fruit martini. Dinner menus, which change daily, were swiftly brought by the waistcoat-clad staff, so we could linger over the choice of seared scallops with pea purée, or Barnsley lamb chop with spinach-and-anchovy sauce. Three hours later, we were still sitting there, still imbibing and having graduated to ordering wines by the glass. The atmosphere was conducive to slow drinking and fast talking – or was it the other way round? Either way, it seemed the ideal balance for an evening in a boutique hotel bar. Finally, we dragged our fun-fatigued, food-full limbs upstairs and flopped into the bed, large enough to allow us to digest in solitary peace. That smart chap at the start of our stay had it right: it was, very, very special, indeed.

Reviewed by Lucy Cleland

NEED TO KNOW

Rooms 14.

Rates From £145–£185 for non-members. Breakfast, from £5.

Check-out 11am, but flexible on request. Earliest check-in, 2pm.

Facilities Games room with table football, private-screening room, DVD library. In rooms, flatscreen TV with Sky+ and DVD player, retro radios, free WiFi, minibar, Cowshed toiletries.

Children Welcome; toys are available in the Playground. Extra beds (£25) or cots (£15) can be added to rooms, but children staying in their own rooms are charged at the full rate.

Also The hotel occupies the top two floors of a building that also houses the renowned High Road Brasserie, as well as a Cowshed boutique, fully stocked with glow-enhancing, skin-pampering and muscle-soothing products.

IN THE KNOW

Our favourite rooms If you have a cat you'd like to swing, the Playroom is the biggest, with zesty lemon and lime accents and a roll-top bath in the bedroom. Tiny and Small are obviously smaller but well designed, and bathed in natural light.

Hotel bar Downstairs at the House is a den-like lounge space with three areas; it's adults-only in the evening, with DJs on Thursday, Friday and Saturday nights. Whisper sweet nothings over an Electric Love Potion cocktail (champagne, vanilla vodka and poached strawberries – divine).

Hotel restaurant Upstairs at the House, kitted out in Ilse Crawford's inimitable retro-modern style, has all-day dining, from breakfast at 7am until wee-hour snacks at the weekend, and a bar. Sit, read, work, eat, drink – it's very easy-going, but a dinner reservation is advisable.

Top table Upstairs, in the space adjacent to the bar; Downstairs, on a huge red sofa in the central Playpen.

Room service The house menu and drinks are available from 7am till 1am (midnight on Sundays).

Dress code The fashionable end of smart casual; Chloé plus Topshop equals just right.

Local knowledge Stroll up Chiswick High Road and pick up a ready-to-go picnic box for two from big-hitting Italian deli and diner Carluccio's (020 8995 8073). Lazybones can potter across to Turnham Green, just opposite; alternatively, the Royal Botanic Gardens at Kew is only two stops away on the District Line (or a short cab ride).

LOCAL EATING AND DRINKING

Combine a stroll along the Thames with lunch or dinner at **Pissarro**, close to Chiswick Pier (020 8994 3111) – ask for a river view and a plate of oysters. Other good evening-meal venues in Chiswick include Parisian-style bistro **Le Vacherin** (020 8742 2121) and luxe French restaurant **La Trompette** (020 8747 1836). In the Barley Mow Centre, **Sam's** (020 8987 0555) is an excellent but unpretentious modern brasserie with imaginative brunch menus and a smart bar. Spice things up in W6 with a tastebud-tantalising thali at **Indian Zing** on King Street (020 8748 5959).

GET A ROOM!

For more information, or to book this hotel, go to www.mrandmrssmith.com. Register your Smith membership card (see pages 4–5) to enjoy exclusive offers and privileges.

SMITH MEMBER OFFER A full-size Cowshed beauty product: Wild Cow, Grumpy Cow or Knackered Cow bath and massage oils.

High Road House 162 Chiswick High Road, London W4 1PR (020 8742 1717; www.highroadhouse.co.uk)

NORFOLK

COUNTRYSIDE A walk on the wild side
COUNTRY LIFE Quiet and quirky

The famous Broads, the wild and wonder-filled beaches, the huge skies: Norfolk is a remote and inspiring corner of England, just a couple of hours from London. This flat-as-a-pancake county is filled with historical houses and untamed countryside, and criss-crossed with active waterways. As well as a wealth of bustling market towns worth a gander, Norfolk also has one of the most fascinating, breathtaking and romantic coastlines in the country. Enjoy dreamy days by the sea, stopping for tea and antiques-browsing; or stray south and step from pastoral idyll into thick evergreens where the wildlife-rich Breckland District cradles Thetford Forest before spilling down into Suffolk. First cultivated in the Twenties as a timber resource, this sprawling patch of pine trees now plays home to endangered British beasties such as red squirrel, golden pheasant and woodlark.

GETTING THERE

Planes Gatwick and Heathrow are two or three hours away by train, via London. There's also an airport at Norwich, with limited but occasionally handy connections (www.norwichairport.co.uk).

Trains Trains leave from London King's Cross for King's Lynn twice an hour; the journey takes about 90 minutes. The half-hourly service from London Liverpool Street to Norwich takes a couple of hours. From Norwich, there are trains to Wroxham (for the Broads), Cromer and Sheringham, where the Coasthopper bus (www.coasthopper.co.uk) will connect you to villages along the north Norfolk coast.

Automobiles The drive from London takes two to three hours via the M11 and A11.

Boats You're unlikely to be using them to go from A to B, but boating on the Broads, especially in the 'executive' vessels, can be fun. Hire for the day and request a picnic.

LOCAL KNOWLEDGE

Taxis Even at train stations, it can be hard to find a cab; ask your hotel to recommend a local firm and book ahead.

Packing tips This is one of the most wonderful places in the UK for wild swimming, so bring your trunks or bikini.

Recommended reads Malcolm Bradbury's classic satire *The History Man* is based on his time as a teacher at the University of East Anglia in Norwich during the Seventies. WG Sebald, who wrote the brilliant *Austerlitz*, also taught at the university.

Local specialities There's lots of game, but best of all is the seafood: Brancaster mussels and Cromer crab are top picks. Sample Norfolk's finest fare at the Saracen's Head in Wolterton (01263 768909), where the menu lists food miles for regional finds. At the Iceni Brewery shop in Ickburgh (www.icenibrewery.co.uk), you can buy bottles of brilliantly monikered local ales Deirdre of the Sorrows, Fine Soft Day or Boudicea Chariot Ale.

Perfect picnic Pick up some fresh bread, local preserves plus whatever's on the daily-changing blackboard at CoCoe's deli and café in Swaffham, then take your moveable feast to enjoy in the wooded gardens at romantic moated mansion Oxburgh Hall (01366 328258).

And... 'Very flat, Norfolk,' as Noël Coward so succinctly said in *Private Lives*. So it's important to know a bit about the tides: they change hundreds of acres of perfect sandy beach into a pretty but pebbly few yards. The BBC's weather webpage is handy for low and high tide times.

WORTH GETTING OUT OF BED FOR

Viewpoint You're not going to climb any mountains in Norfolk, but Gun Hill, west of Holkham Bay, gives a beautiful panorama across land and sea.

Arts and culture Norfolk history is everywhere you look, from the beaches where Nelson played as a boy to the 16th-century brothel that is now the gentrified Hoste Arms in the twee village of Burnham Market – nicknamed Chelsea-on-Sea. As well as Sandringham (the Queen's country retreat, so check when it's open: 01553 612908), Holkham Hall at Wells-next-the-Sea (01328 710227) and Felbrigg Hall just outside Norwich (01263 837444) will provide satisfyingly stuffy days out with cream teas, antiques-packed rooms and beautiful gardens. The Ecotech Centre (01760 726100; www.ecotech.org.uk) is set in extensive grounds, an organically managed area revealing all you need to know about sustainability. Norfolk has 646 mediaeval churches – a greater density than anywhere else in the world – so choose which ones you'd like to visit at www.norfolkopenchurches.com.

Daytripper Head down to Bury St Edmunds for the day, a mediaeval town that rivals Bath for its golden Georgian buildings and Roman roots. Explore the abbey ruins and the age-old Guildhall, and the markets if you've visited on a Wednesday or Saturday.

Activities Old Hunstanton beach – fondly referred to as 'Sunny Hunny' as it is the only east coast town that faces west – is often deserted on land, but is the perfect location for kitesurfing. Lovers of this sport might also want to earmark Brancaster, seven miles east along the coast. Alternatively, dabble in archery, bushcraft or wild swimming on a kayaking expedition in the Broads National Park (www.thecanoeman.com).

Children Pack a kite to fly on one of the many beaches or take the kids seal-spotting on a trip to Blakeney Point. Beans Boat Trips (www.beansboattrips.co.uk) set off from Morston (of mussels fame) near Cley, or Blakeney Quay, and take you right up to the action: a 500-strong colony of common and grey seal basking on the sand.

Walks Set off from Overstrand, a cliff-top village in the east, at low tide and walk for an hour or so along the coast to Cromer; the sweeping views won't disappoint. If you're a bit of a twitcher, grab your binoculars and go on a bird-spotting circuit around Blakeney Freshes: start in the village, head down to the quay and then follow the footpath towards the harbour and back around and down to the Coast Road. In the summer, keep your eyes open for marsh harrier, red shank, breeder wading birds and Chinese water deer.

Shopping Most towns have a market at least once a week: Cromer's is on Fridays, Sheringham market is Wednesdays and Saturdays, and Swaffham has an antiques market on Saturdays. Holt is another hotspot for time-worn trinkets. In Norwich, the Lanes is brilliant boutique-browsing territory; we love independent fashion store Walkers of Pottergate (01603 618718). Norwich Market is the largest six-day market in the UK, and has stood here on the same site since the 11th century (www.visitnorwich.co.uk).

Something for nothing The beaches along the north Norfolk coast are well known and well loved for their beauty and romance. Take a blanket and picnic (or just a bottle of something good) and find your own quiet spot among the dunes. (You can't go far wrong with the vast sprawl of sand where Holkham National Nature Reserve hits the coast.)

Don't go home without... seeing the rainbow of beach huts dotted along the beach at Wells-next-the-Sea – the colourful cubes will brighten any cloudy sky. If you're averse to donning swimwear, naturists should seek out the nudist beach to the west of Holkham.

NATURALLY NORFOLK

What do Norfolk Nog, Nelson's Revenge, Tipples' Redhead, Hanged Monk and Reedcutter have in common? No, they're not emo-pop tribute bands: they're ales and bitters that hail from this county (it comes second only to West Yorkshire for beer production). The Campaign For Real Ale even claims its 31 breweries in fact make Norfolk the best place to enjoy a pint.

DIARY

Late April Newmarket's 1,000 Guineas Stakes is one of the season's classic flat races (www.newmarketracecourses.co.uk). **May** The Crab & Lobster Festival is a weekend celebration of the coastal towns of Sheringham and Cromer, with events including arts and crafts shows (www.crabandlobsterfestival.co.uk). The international programme of music, theatre, dance, circus, outdoor performances and visual arts at the Norfolk & Norwich Festival attracts thousands in that same third week of May (www.nnfestival.org.uk). **August** Cromer Carnival is a proper English village affair, with floats, bands and fireworks (www.cromercarnival.co.uk).